Beelzebub's Bargain

Beelzebub's Bargain

Published and Copyrighted 2011
by Ronald Scheckelhoff,

211 Dutchess Dr., Cary, NC, 27513

Art graciously provided by the waters of
Jordan Lake, in North Carolina

Graphics by Ronald Scheckelhoff

ISBN 978-0-9849656-2-5
Library of Congress control # 2011963286

Author/Publisher DBA:

Kristen's Tree Publishing

(Distributor for trade shows/book fairs)

First release printing (novelette version)

Jan 18th, 2012

Flashback

Lindsay Kidde was good - damned good, and it didn't matter which proprietary cell phone operating system he was handed. His exceptional ability to pour out complex source code, for any system, was legendary. He could do it better than other topnotch byte smiths could code Unix, Linux, or Windows. That's why he had become a special projects and prototype setup man for MagintorCorp Cellular.

Lindsay had just finished his most recent setup. It had been a queer one, for certain. The room at MagintorCorp, tucked into a corner on the eleventh floor, looked much like any police station interrogation room, with a large table in the center, two chairs, and an expanse of one-way glass across the narrow end of the room. Now he stood next to one of the figures behind the glass, waiting. He had been told to stay until it could be determined that the setup had been done correctly. Not that Lindsay's work ever needed to be redone. The man's perfectionism matched his work record - and it was rarely tarnished.

Lindsay watched as the young woman entered the room. The thin man who accompanied her into the room, asked her to take a seat at one of the chairs that had been pushed up next to the table. His voice could be heard clearly over the speaker mounted high on the wall, behind the glass. "OK," he said, "now you can do what we talked about. Call your mother." The tall thin man smiled, and left the room.

The woman shook her head, as if to say that it was a mighty strange day indeed that found official looking men in expensive suits paying her five hundred dollars to talk with her mother. That was something she did often for free. Strange, but welcome, and so the temp agency girl dialed the number she knew so well.

Lindsay watched the woman chat, and soon the banter was a high pitched cadence of mother-daughter talk, with nary a syllable's length of silence, interspersed here and there, to break it up.

The project manager - the one who had given Lindsay the orders to stay put, picked up another cell phone. It was the phone that Lindsay had modified, per the special project leader's request. "Pat the top of your head." he said. The woman did as she was asked, never breaking the cadence of her fast paced dialog, never changing her demeanor at all. She just kept on talking.

Now the project leader turned to Lindsay, "It looks like all is in order here. Your work is as your boss described. Flawless. That is all we need from you today. Thank you Mr. Kidde."

1

Barry

Barry squeezed Alicia's hand tightly as the twosome rounded the corner and started out on the last leg of the street that meandered out of their neighborhood. The brisk evening air seemed cooler than the wind breaker jackets they donned on the way out of the apartment. As they mounted the high spot on the ridge, they were afforded a clear view of the surrounding city, and the jam of apartments clustered everywhere they could see. The voice wafted over the rooftops of the buildings that covered the low-lying westward section that lay ahead of them. The couple looked at one another, each face primed to posit a question, unsure of what it should be. They walked a hundred yards further, descending to a flat section of the road, and another voice came along to them in the cold wind. The answer to the first call chanted the same words. Up overhead, the sinking sky smothered them with the dark gray drabness of a late Northern fall evening. The north wind stretched the sound of the voices, blending them to eerie wisps ...

Barry pulled Alicia more tightly into his side. He changed the course of their evening walk – maneuvering the bonded four legged creature they had become deftly off of the road and down onto a bike-way trail. The trail descended sharply, losing fifty feet inside of two hundred paces, until it had aligned itself next to a small-trickle creek bed. The huddled couple continued down into the deeply greened and shadowed enclave of the wild area, an unexpected encroachment on the inner city, as it prematurely slipped from dusk to darkness.   The wind could not reach down into the little swatch of briar and forest.   Ahead of them a small bench partially obtruded the weedy path.   Likely placed there by city workers too many years before, its surface was pithy and rough, its center cradled like an old grandmother's mattress.   Still, it must have been a fortuitous find for many a weary hiker.

They sat in silence for a long while, leaning against each other. The rustling of some small animal finally shook both of them into sharp focus again.   "What is this place?" Alicia finally put out just over the top of her breath. In a tone of one who does not believe, Barry responded only a little more firmly than Licia had, "Just another little city in the heartland?"

Smitty

They reentered the apartment, and   tossed each of their lightweight jackets onto the ceramic hooks nailed to the side of the pantry. An hour later, sitting at the table, the twosome had resumed their inward, quiet postures.   A slurp of spaghetti finally coached a corner smile from Alicia and jostled Barry from his silence.   "The guys at the station seem alright," he said. "I mean ... they seem fairly normal to me - whatever that is.   The captain's pretty cool, I think.   But yeah, the neighborhood is a little queer.   Nothing like back home in Wisconsin."

"Maybe some of the strangeness of this place has to do with its size.   This is a big city ... something you and I aren't very familiar with. Maybe, when you have so many people together in one place, like it is here, you're more likely to notice the crazies.   If, as a matter of demographics, three out of a hundred people are just plain crazy, then living in a village having only a thousand people doesn't put you in touch with very many of them. Remember crazy Smitty?" Alicia started laughing, and Barry added an outburst. "He was a trip."

"It may be that we just have a whole lot more of the Smitty types around here. It might take some getting used to."

They moved to a small family room, adjacent to the kitchen. Barry thumbed the remote control through a dozen channels. "Not much on the tube." Licia waved her paperback book around in the air, "That's why I buy novels like this one, couch potato."

"We should just disconnect the thing. It puts such a whooping on my my patrolman's salary. Then maybe we'd have a little more dough for other things."

"Like a new dress every month?" Barry smiled. "You can have a new dress anytime you want."

Alicia finished her chapter. It didn't matter that it was a quarter till one. She always finished her chapters. It was just one of those things she needed to do – it marked a quirk that was one of her very few out-of-character dimensions. It was that one thing she simply had to carry to the point of obsessive compulsiveness – like skipping cracks in the sidewalk might be for other people.

Barry was already under the sheets by the time Alicia walked into the bedroom. Lying on his side, he watched her undress. She pulled away her sweater and her undergarments, and let them drop into the laundry net that hung on the tubular frame in the corner of the room. Barry turned his eyes back to the alarm clock on her side of the bed. The deep red of the old style LED reflected from the top of the nightstand, and the numbers displayed the time: one fifteen A.M. He knew well how unwise it would be to watch her so closely in these wee hours – lest he not get any sleep at all.

Her near perfect form slipped under the sheets, blotting out the reflections of the LED display, and gently bouncing the mattress under Barry as she curled up on it. She faced away from him, as always, as she had done every single night for the past two years ... every night that had passed since the awful night that changed their lives ... that sent him in one direction and her in another ... that had torn their world apart.

He draped his arm over Alicia's side, and it brushed her soft skin close to her breast. "Please," she whispered. Barry pulled his hand back. He rolled over onto his back. "Sleep now," he said to himself, "tomorrow promises to be a long day."

The Meeting

Alicia made coffee for Barry. It was hot to go, along with the eggs and the bacon. Barry was impressed. Alicia was not one to rise early or to make breakfast for herself – yet alone someone else. "Thanks!" he smiled over the top of his cup. "I'll get there on time today. The big shots will be impressed." Alicia laughed, "Great attitude for someone with less than a month's time on the force!"

Barry kissed his wife on the forehead, grabbed his windbreaker, and slipped out of the door.

Barry beat his sidekick Kersh to the locker room, and his month long road patrol companion mentioned this. "Waddya – try'in to get a raise?" Barry shook his head, "Nah, the wife got up early to fix my grits." Kersh's face slipped into a mischievous smile, "Appreciation breakfast, huh? Way to go bucko!" Barry smiled, "She's just a great gal. From what you tell me, you don't know any of those."

"Yeah – remind me, why dontcha?"

The two patrolmen sat through the "big meeting" that had been promised the day before. As they exited the room, Kersh breathed out his sentence and yawned at the same time, "In a word: anticlimactic." Barry's expression indicated full concordance with his sidekick. As they reached the squad car, Barry lamented, "No donuts either, and they claim this is a police station." The first stop was made without any further dialog. The squad car's brakes squealed as Kersh pulled into the narrow slot next to the van with the gaudy orange lettering on the side, formed into an advertisement for L&S Vending Company. "See," said Kersh, "it's not only us policemen who slink into these places. I'll bet you can guess who drives that truck." Barry looked through the window of the business as he shook his head, "He must go three and a quarter - maybe three fifty if he goes an ounce. He must sample his L&S snacks and this stuff too!" The overweight man with the faded L&S letters on his uniform occupied the last barstool at the counter, sipping his coffee. As this impressive man launched a premium sized donut into the opening above his jowls, Barry glanced at his companion, and turned to the clerk behind the counter. "I'll have a small donut and coffee – black as you can make it."

"No fritter today?" Barry shook his head, "I dunno – I seem to feel motivated to change up a little today. "

The squad car and its donut toting occupants had just pulled out onto the boulevard when the radio cackled out its accident description. Kersh bumped the knob on the radio, "Hey, that's one of our guys. What does the console say?" Barry looked down at the console, "Yup – officer's from our precinct. It says it's patrolman Jere - "

"Jere!" Kersh interrupted. Let's go!"   Kersh hit the siren button, and pushed down on the pedal. The squad car reeled around the corner at the bottom of the hill, then picked up speed rapidly as it pulled out into the fast lane and headed up towards the midtown bridge.

Three other squad cars were there already, but the ambulance had yet to arrive. Three officers stood next to the wrecked car, watching the bloodied officer.   "There's really nothing we can do. He's gone." Barry winced as his eyes pulled the scene into his brain. The front third of the officer's head had been crushed and pushed back into a flat slope, starting at the top of the head, and continuing down to the top of his exposed teeth. Material trickled from his broken chin down onto his leg, where a small pile of the had accumulated.

Barry no longer looked at the officer's horrific smashed countenance. Now he stared at the windshield. It was fractured in a small round area, perhaps the size of a fifty cent piece, and many cracks ran out from its center point like twisted bicycle spokes, centered approximately where the officer's head would have made contact. Still, he stared at the spot. The windshield had not shattered. Why had it not shattered? Barry looked at Kersh and then pointed to the windshield's small damaged section. His words came out loudly - "That – didn't do -- that!" Barry moved his pointed finger from the windshield back to the officer.

Before Kersh could answer, he was interrupted by the spitting stones and the blare of the ambulance as it swept into the area next to the tree. That tree was planted partially in the squad car's grill. The police officer in charge of the scene signaled to the bystanders – pushing them back from the grisly scene ...

Later, the twosome sat on a bench in the patrolman's locker room and packed their carry-along bags. "You didn't know Jere, of course. He was a great guy. He always made jokes when the captain asked him to cut his hair. He liked to push the envelope and wear it just a little longer than the regs, you know. Jere would say "The captain thinks my hair is too poofy. We always laughed at this big guy using the word poofy to refer to his hair. Then, there was the time at the policeman's picnic, which happened to be an Oktoberfest of sorts. It was without beer though, which was odd. Guess the department didn't want to pay for it. Anyway, old Jere got up on stage in his lederhosen and played the air accordion. We all nearly died laughing. Great guy."

"Something was wrong with that whole setup, Kersh. It seemed wrong to me, like the scene was forged. Maybe somebody wanted to get even with Jere for a bust." Kersh looked at Barry and paused.

"Ya know, we'll just have to wait and see what they decide. It shouldn't take too long."

Dumplings

Alicia had made apple dumplings for Barry's dessert. Barry loved anything apple. Alicia had told her mother once that, "I could put apples in sawdust and bake it, and Barry would eat it and say it was scrumptious." Barry knew what she was doing. It made it hard for him not to love her, in spite of how it had been for so long. Maybe things would change.

Over dinner, the two talked about Jere and Alicia listened to Barry's lament about the crowd at the accident scene. "I mean

- I use the term "accident" loosely. It didn't seem like one. The real kick in the butt though - was the other officers indifference to the evidence. It's like they couldn't see it ... like it wasn't obvious to them. I mean, it's true that I'm the one with the community college degree in forensic science, I admit. But, this was readily apparent to me. I'd see it without any forensic training. It's absurd Alicia. They weren't paying any attention to obvious things. It was like a movie with bad acting - like Rotten Tomatoes, but with gore."

At half past one, Alicia hadn't finished her chapter. Barry decided to go to bed. Maybe sleep would help him forget the day's horrors. His sleep turned into a dream about his day - one that went on and on and that ended with a slow phantasmagoria, stopping finally with a still frame image of Jere's horrifically mutilated face. It jolted him awake. Rolling over, he regained his sleep, but the nightmare repeated - again and again. Finally, at half past three, exhaustion put him to sleep.

Two days later

It was six forty five A.M. when Barry brought his coffee into the locker room. Kersh noted the convenience store *Java Junky* labeling on the side of it, and advised "You're slipping young man," as he pointed to the cup.

Barry normally would smile, but for two nights on end he had not slept but two hours. "Yeah - it's not Alicia, it's me. I keep having dreams about Jere. They're just awful. Have you heard anything from the captain about this?"

"Nope. Not a word."

The twosome ran through a fairly routine morning patrol,

stopping at a department store to lecture a shoplifter. Between that and the donut stop, it had been uneventful. They returned to the station at one o'clock, and Barry made straight for the captain's door. It was ajar, and he stuck his head into it. "Patrolman Stewart! Problem?"

"Just a question. What was the disposition of the accident involving Jere?" There was a long pause from the captain. Finally, "It was ruled an accidental death by the coroner. Why do you ask?"

"It seemed to indicate something else to me."

"What?"

"The damage to the windshield didn't match up with what happened to Jere, in my opinion."

The captain stood up, "Well, Barry, the chief and the coroner both concurred that the death was accidental. Let's go to the evidence garage, so you can show me why you say what you say."

The captain punched the code into the lock, opened the door, and hit the lights. The vehicle was there, along with two others involved in an evidence chain of one type or another. Barry immediately walked to the side of the patrol car that was Jere's last ride. He stood there looking at the windshield. The captain walked up behind him. "Barry, may I ask why this makes you suspicious?" Barry said nothing. Feeling a coolness on the nape of his neck, he looked at the captain, and shook his head.

"Maybe I'm mistaken captain. Maybe I remembered it wrong."

The captain shrugged, turned to the door and gestured for

Barry to lead them back out into the hallway.

HiJax

HiJax was upscale, by all appearances. It was the place of the sex netters, and Schmidt sat in a booth on one end, sipping one of the fourteen inch glass, foam topped beverages that gave the tavern its name. The sex netters came here to talk business, and needed to keep out the riff-raff. They did this mostly with the exorbitant pricing that non sex netters had to pay. Schmidt tapped the table with his fingers, drumming out a beat, wondering where his appointment was.

When two guys near the door gave out a slew of cat calls, Schmidt knew his appointment had arrived. The woman strode past the whistlers, spun around, and made a great fanfare of bending over to pick up a piece of paper lying on the floor. More cat-calls ensued. Now, the shapely miniskirt clad woman danced over to Schmidt's table, and slid into the booth opposite him.

Schmidt looked at the pretty face, now partially hidden behind a HiJax mug. Your particular expertise is needed to take care of some potential trouble – and a potential troublemaker."

"What trouble?"

"Well, the trouble has a name. Barry Stewart."

"The new guy. Hey – he's kinda cute." Schmidt cocked his head to the side and lowered his voice, saying – "You need to get all the extracurricular baloney out of your head. This is business, and it needs to be done right."

"You know me. I'm the business girl."

"Good. I want this done as soon as possible. He usually

checks into the station just after noon.   You'll be there when he is."

Forensics

Barry Stewart had his wife's sympathy when he poked his head into the apartment.   The toll of three near sleepless nights was etched all over his face.   Over dinner, the conversation was mostly about Jere's car and its windshield. He replayed the trip to the evidence garage, and the feelings that gripped him when he saw that the windshield was missing – completely shattered. It was not only the windshield that bugged him, but also the fact that the damage to the front of the vehicle was not extensive. It bugged him that the air bags had not gone off.   He knew that a high velocity impact with a even a safety glass windshield might kill, but there was absolutely no way that it could have done what was done – to Jere.   Of this, he was certain.

"Schmidt, Graham, and Elliot were the patrolmen at the accident scene before I arrived.   They should never have believed that the scene was legit.   And then – there's what happened in the evidence garage.   It makes no sense to me."

Alicia followed her husband to bed early, forgoing the usual after dinner book and the full chapter that was her almost uncompromisable habit. Just before he fell asleep, he felt the touch of her hand on his shoulder. She hadn't done that in a long while.

2

Vice

Kersh pointed at the van as the brakes squealed, and they made the first stop of the day. "The man's pushing the envelope in my opinion." Barry smiled, "That's not all he's pushing."

They had a quiet couple of donuts, and Barry's mood was as black as the coffee. He gave up on having a dialog with Kersh about the Jere incident. "The smart boys have it all figured out," was about all Kersh would say. "The coroner looks at this stuff all day long – so do the detectives. I'll tell you one thing Barry. In this department you will have to go along to get along. The free thinkers get drummed out pretty quickly. Actually, Jere was a good guy – everybody agrees. But, he was one of those free-thinker types. That's why, when he died, he had the exact same position as when he entered the department twenty years ago. He was an entry level patrolman, basically his entire career.

The day was fairly uneventful, excepting for a speeder who wanted to play the line right on the edge relative to an eluding a police officer charge. Kersh flipped the lights on, but not the siren, a routine procedure when in heavy traffic so as not to cause accidents with nearby vehicles. The speeder knew he was the intended recipient of a ticket and dodged off on another street while adding a little more speed to what was already too much. He went about half a mile in this fashion, until finally Kersh hit the siren button and put the patrol car a fly speck's space away from the guy's rear bumper. In spite of all the crap and a belligerent attitude, he gave the man a regular ticket. "Too much paperwork."

When Barry walked into the station just after one, Kersh headed off to the lunch room. Elliot was waving from the opening of the captain's door, motioning for Barry to walk over to him. Barry was disinclined, but Elliot did seem to have the captain's ear. Elliot came across with that big tooth sort of smile that Barry had learned to distrust.

"Captain here says I can borrow you after lunch. Seems the precinct has been pretty devoid of paying enthusiasts, so little Officer Cindi needs a lift over to precinct 13. Captain says you're the man for the job." Then, in a lower tone voiced out of the side of his mouth, he said, "We're all jealous. Most of us would haul Cindi's tail anywhere."

"You'll find her in the lunch room." A few moments later, Barry emerged from the break room with officer Cindi in tow. The two of them walked down the steps of precinct 3 headquarters, and out to the lot where the transport van was located. The destination was about six miles - up and over the midtown bridge, and then along the river for a couple more miles. As they rode, officer Cindi played with the hem of her dress - fussing with it. Barry noticed this out of the corner of his eye, and he noticed that the regular training laps at the police exercise track had done her no harm. Finally he asked, "Is there a problem?" Officer Cindi looked at him and slowly shook her head. Barry read Cindi's mischievous grin and her quick glance to the back of the windowless van as a single complete thought. He felt the tinge of a rush, but his carnal impulse was overshadowed by days spent observing the strange doings of stranger people. Mentally, he added Cindi's name to the list of actors and actresses. This was the *B movie* sequence where Barry would fall, inexplicably, for a clumsy setup. Barry ignored Cindi's hand as its gesture invited him to the empty parking lot along the street. "Not happening today sweet pea." Barry knew that he had made his doubts about the Jere matter very public, and it was Elliot who had commandeered his afternoon to make this special trip. Was it as obvious as it seemed that the comely vice officer Cindi's name should be added to the short list of people he shouldn't trust? Where did this list end? Barry was beginning to regret the move from Milwaukee.

"So, you and Elliot set this up to waste my afternoon and make fun of the new guy?"

"Elliot's an idiot. He puts on those silly blue suspenders and then thinks he is Elliot Ness. He's not very bright, you know. I just think you are cute ... and smart ... unlike Elliot, and I know about your troubles with your wife."

"Great. My loyal sidekick can't keep a secret. I'll need to remember that. Well, you're wrong about my wife. I love her, and any problems we have are not related to that. It's really not anybody else's business no matter what it is. Truthfully, you're being a bit of a skank."

Cindi looked dourly at Barry. "Crap. The one time I risk making a fool of myself I'm successful. It's not like I do this all the time." Barry looked at her with an expression that broadcasted his doubts pretty succinctly.

Barry shook his head, "You'll have to find your own boyfriend. I have already been fished."

Therapy

Barry and Alicia took their usual walk to their secret little enclave, and sat together on their crooked little bench. "Tomorrow is our support group meeting," Alicia whispered after Barry had talked through a description of his work day. He left Cindi completely out of the mostly one sided conversation. "Yes, I know. We missed the last one, didn't we?"

Later, at dinner, Barry was moody. To Alicia it was obvious that his mind was occupied with something – maybe work related - and so she retired to the corner sofa and the book lying on the lamp-stand next to it.

Barry's night was restless. A person, seemingly foreign to Barry's memory, appeared in his dream. The dream went on and on with its fuzzy detail and its ambiguity, but his mind perceived it as non-threatening, and allowed him to sleep. It changed his nocturnal rhythm, as it was the first night that Jere's face did not appear to him. In the morning, the couple took their late, quick breakfast, as was their habit on support group mornings. Most officers would not parry the leverage needed to break a Saturday free to be at home, but the department made an exception for Barry and his wife. Given the horror of her ordeal two years before, the chief had deemed it the sensible thing to do. Most of the other department members concurred, even though it meant an occasional extra weekend shift for them. The brutal rape of his wife was the reason for Barry to join the force as a patrolman.

At ten forty five, Barry pulled his Volvo into the parking space at the center, and the twosome made their way to the second building and its second floor room, down on the end of the hallway. The usual crew was there, and the usual ritual exercised, starting with the ice-breaker round robin for the new group members.

Alicia was always more at ease with herself on the trips home after the sessions. Barry thought – that with time – she might learn to trust people, and to disassociate that which was a bad memory from that which is current and that could be good again. She was recovering from a trauma to the brain – in some ways, perhaps, the same as a physical trauma. Each passing day and each additional session gave Barry more hope that Alicia would be well again. The couple took a lunch at a new place, something they did to celebrate the progress of each session and step. Barry had his usual turkey salad, and Alicia scolded him, as usual, for eating turkey. Alicia had always been a vegetarian but – coming from Wisconsin – she could never be a vegan.

Darla

The middle aged woman answered Barry's knock. She was dressed in lively colors, far removed from the dark ones that surely shrouded her heart. She even managed a hint of a smile as she pulled the door fully open and let Barry into her little bungalow. Mrs. Goodwin pointed to a chair in the corner. "That was his favorite, and I'm sure he would want a fellow officer to sit in it now."

Barry lowered himself into the well worn recliner, situated so that it had the room's command view of the television. "I want to extend my sympathies to you, Mrs. Goodwin, about Jere," he said after the widow took a spot on the sofa.

"Thank you."

"I'm sorry to say I did not know your husband very well. I have been on the force for only a couple months now, and he worked mostly in another precinct."

Mrs. Goodwin nodded. "I'm glad you stopped by. The first

week or so, I was, as you might imagine, overwhelmed. Many of Jere's fellow officers came around – but due to the circumstances I can't say that I remember much of what they had to say, excepting for a few of his closest colleagues.

Now, I'm trying not to be morose or melancholy all of the time, because I know Jere wouldn't want me to be that way. He was always upbeat about things."

Barry looked at Mrs. Goodwin, and his smile dropped a little, "I know you're still grieving for your husband, and I don't want to upset you in any way. However; I must say something in order to follow up on issues that could relate to your husband's death. Mainly, I was one of those at the accident scene, and I find that I don't agree with the coroner's decision on the matter of your dear husband's death. So, Mrs Goodwin-" "Just call me Darla," the widow interjected. Now she held her face up, and she looked squarely into Barry's eyes.

"What do you mean – when you say you don't agree with the coroner?"

Barry crossed his feet in front of the recliner. He looked down at the floor for a few moments. When he looked up, his face had transformed in a way meant to impart a reassuring smile – to put Darla at ease and not provoke alarm or add to her emotional turmoil.

"You've been through a lot lately, Darla. I'm not here to put any more on your shoulders. I'm not sure what I think about the situation. I'd like to ask you some questions that maybe will help me to understand what I don't. In the last few months of his life, did you notice any changes in Jere? Was he the same person you've always known? Were there any changes in routine? Did he pick up new habits or exhibit any mood changes?"

"My God. You're not saying he committed suicide?!"

"No, nothing of the sort."

Darla said nothing for a while, and then she got up off of the sofa and turned towards the kitchen that adjoined the living room. "Can I get you anything to drink patrolman Stewart?" "A soda maybe?" "That would be fine," answered Barry. He could hear the cupboard doors as Darla opened and closed them. In his mind he could see her slow, deliberate motions as she pulled the glasses down, and turned to open the fridge. It seemed to Barry that she was formulating her answer, trying to decide what to say and how to say it.

"You can just call me Barry," he said as Darla handed him the glass.

Darla sat down, this time picking a spot closer to her late husband's favorite chair and the young police officer sitting in it. "While I was pouring your soda, I thought about what you said about Jere. You know, with the accident report and the coroner's certificate, I really never gave any thought to anything like the questions you asked me. I mean, I had no reason to think about how Jere was ... it didn't occur to me."

Darla paused, and it was obvious to Barry that she was cycling through items in her mind – through things related to Jere. Finally, Darla resumed, "In the last few months, Jere was not himself. He was not, as you say, the man I've known so many years. He was always such an exuberant and jovial person – sometimes to the point of being irritating when I wasn't in the mood for some of his silliness. We had our down moments, but our spats never lasted very long. We were quick maker-uppers." Darla pulled in a long breath. "You know, his demeanor really did seem to change after he was nominated to be a sex netter."

Barry looked at Darla for an uncomfortable few moments of silence, with the facial expression of a person who could not decode the message. Darla looked up and smiled. She almost laughed as she realized that Barry might not know about the sex netters.

"It's really not about sex – it's a play on the letters they use to describe the group of officers – and some of the others involved. I can't remember what it stands for exactly now – but it's security related. "Safe, Secure in Every Community" - yeah, that's it – or something like that. Anyway, he was nominated to be one of the liaison officers.

At first, it seemed like any of those token nominations that the boss might give you as part of a morale boosting program. He had never really been promoted beyond where he started, and he thought his boss was giving him a feather to stick in his hat – a little esprit de corps.

Shortly after he started with the program, he began staying out late, which was very unusual and strange for him. He was not part of any unit that would do stake outs, really, but he used that as the reason for the late nights. I didn't have a reason to question him, but the change in his mood troubled me. I associated it with the stake outs, which of course have the potential to be dangerous. I thought about how he didn't want to say anything to me about the case he was working on. This was an odd thing, because --- *I don't know how it is with your wife, Barry, but I think policemen often confide things to spouses*, even when these things are officially under wraps. Some things are just too much to keep inside, and so they trust their spouses to keep the secret. When you have a certain kind of relationship, there are no secrets, and there are no disclosures either. He would often let things slip - almost unconsciously - and I picked them up because I knew him so well. You know – it's the way it is when you constantly complete each other's sentences. But, he was absolutely mum about the stake outs he was doing. He didn't even mumble anything about it. The whole thing was absolutely taboo in our conversation. He didn't say anything about the sex netters either, which was weird. I mean, what could be so secretive about a community liaison activity? I thought that was a little strange, but I shrugged it away."

Barry took all of her comments in without saying anything. An old policeman's trick, learned as part of some forensic class. When they get started, you let them go. It's the rhythm that breaks the secrets, although he was certain that Darla was telling the story as best she could.

"Did he have any new habits?" he inquired. Darla looked a little distressed, then she said "He was hanging out with the sex netters at HiJax. It's a bar. I was worried that he might be trying to take solace in the wrong thing – you know – alcohol. That was not something he'd ever done before, as far as I know, and it was troubling."

...

The doorbell rang, and Darla went to answer. An attractive, petite young woman – perhaps Barry's age or younger – entered the bungalow.

"Barry, I'd like you to meet Rose Engleman. She's a friend of mine. I had completely forgotten that we were going to do something tonight. I'm sorry, but we're supposed to be at the place in a half hour." Barry stood up and walked over to Darla.

"It has been very informative for me, Darla. May I visit again if I have other questions?" Darla nodded, and she and her friend Rose shook his hand before he turned to walk out of the door.

"Maybe they sell more than beer here," mused Barry as he stepped up on the sidewalk in front of the bar. Darkness had almost completely descended onto the street out front, and the sign hanging over the door did little to counteract it. Only the bulbs under the syllable "Hi" were lit, and the Jax portion was dark.

The crowd was sparse, so Barry found a table with an advantageous view close to the over-sized HDTV screen, tuned to a local game.

The barkeep walked to Barry's table and asked him what he wanted. "I'll have a lemon lime soda - no ice." A minute later, the burly man with the apron planted a tall glass of soda on the table. "That's eight bucks." Barry looked at the man and smiled, reached around and pulled two dollars from his wallet. The barkeep crossed his arms. "Ain't gonna do it. It's eight bucks. Really." Barry reached again for his wallet. Just as he pulled it out, a voice came from a table in the far corner of the barroom. "Hey! That's a fellow police officer," Schmidt shouted from his table. "He should get the usual discount." The burly man stepped back from the table and feigned a slap to the head, as if to say, "What was I thinking?" "It's only seven seventy five after the discount." The crowd, mostly gathered around a table close to the door, burst into laughter. Barry handed the man a ten spot. "If you people don't want certain kinds of patrons, why don't you make it a private club and hire a bouncer?" The burly man turned to the crowd and waved his arms around in the air. "Because," he said, "We're all bouncers!" The crowd again burst into laughter.

Barry shook his head, got up from his table, and moved to the bar. "Doesn't matter if you change seats - the ticker starts when I give you the drink. We serve another one after thirty minutes." Again, the burly barkeep waved his hands in the air. "How else do we ensconce your personage within such ambiance as this?" The table near the door exploded with a combination of cackles and guffaws.

Barry decided to leave his almost full glass of soda, but he stiffened his legs around the seat of the stool instead. At the back side of the barroom, he noticed two men - each sitting at separate tables. They seemed to be looking at nothing at all, staring mostly into the emptiness at the center of the barroom, seemingly oblivious to the noise and everything else around them, yet putting out an aura that suggested something else, such as being the unofficial, but discrete proctors of the scene.

There came a banging noise from the door on the side of the barroom, down just a few feet from the end of the bar. Barry hadn't noticed it before, but now he realized that it was an exit more convenient to his car whenever he might be ready to terminate his little mission. He wanted to do that without any further insult or delay. The barkeep opened the side door, and spoke briefly with someone outside. He turned to look at Barry as he spoke. He closed the door and Barry went back to feigning interest in a local game showing on the small screen above and behind the bar.

Barry looked down at the ten spot he had placed under his glass in anticipation of the next scheduled mugging. His reverie was broken by a furry paw of a hand - one that was attached to the burly apron wearer - and which reached for the ten spot and pulled it out from under the glass.

"We treat our real drinkers better," came from the man who

had taken possession of his money. "If you'll order a man's drink, it'll be for free this time." Barry had no reason to waste another ten clams, so he shook his head, "I'll have an Old Dutch in a bottle then." The barkeep smiled and nodded. As he did so, Barry noticed the man's partial set of teeth would require serious work before any family photo session. One jagged tooth on the left side was capped in gold, and Barry wondered how it might be that a man could afford a gold cap for one tooth, yet lose most of the others. The burly one reached towards Barry with his hairy fist, and jammed the ten spot into Barry's shirt pocket. "Old Dutch it is!" he exclaimed.

The company's icon stood tall above the quadrangle in front of its corporate headquarters building. The black suited men slipped under the giant tiger sculpture, past the line of trees on the perimeter of the property, flashing something to the guard in the shack as they passed the little booth. Briskly, they walked up to the entry doors at the base of the seven story building.

The most executive office - that of the company's topmost officer, was guarded by his secretary, and her appointment schedule. Mr. Dennison's secretary greeted the two men as they entered the reception area outside of his office. "We are here to see Mr. Dennison." The secretary glanced at the LCD monitor on her desk. "I have no appointments for the president this morning. You must be mistaken." The taller of the two men pulled back the button side of his suit, displaying a badge. Pulling it from the shirt clip, he handed it to Ms. Lauren. The secretary started reading the badge number, half aloud, "10RZL8BW141 ... "

"This means nothing to me," she said finally. The tall one spoke again, saying "We are from the department of-" when his voice was silenced by the noisy door of the executive suite, as it opened. Mr. Dennison stepped outside of the office. "Is there a problem?"

Mr. Dennison normally carried the permanent smile that is typical of those who get elected president. Now it turned into a frown. "You again. Well, I haven't changed my mind."

"Lynn, please clear out a fifteen minute session in the schedule. By the end of that time, these two will be leaving."

The secretary nodded, and Dennison curtly waved the two men into the office, pulling the door closed behind himself as he reentered it.

"It's a matter of the security of our people, Mr. Dennison. It's not that we like to bother you or take you away from your other appointments." Tony, the tall one, turned to his associate, "He's a busy man, isn't he?" The latter replied, with just a hint of a smirk, "Surely he is."

Dennison stood up and walked to the window. "What you are asking me to do serves my company and my clients in no way. My own engineers cannot fathom a purpose for what you requested. It does not benefit Sky Tiger Cellular, Inc., in any way that I can see. It's not even a technically reasonable thing to do. It has no purpose, in the eyes of my technical staff. You want me to add a data object to the stream, and provise it to generate simulated analog echoes from our customer's phones. Ludicrous! What for? When I ask you, and I get the old "It's a security issue bag of rot." No real answers that my quite talented engineers can believe. Our equipment no longer processes analog signals anyway, so there would never be a way to use your network wasting bandwidth for any actual communications. It's just ridiculous, unless it's part of some of your agency's hanky panky, and nothing else. Eventually, when it's discovered that you're doing something to abridge my client's privacy – I get blamed for it. No – it's worse than that - my company gets blamed for it, and we go out of business."

"Gentlemen, you're fifteen minutes has expired." Dennison picked up the phone. "George, I need an escort to help a couple of our visitors to find the door."

3

Echoes

Geo Dennison's daughter paced the floor. It was not like her dad to miss one of her school dances. He was her ride to school, and it was unimaginable that he would let her down. Kristen was daddy's pride and joy.

George pushed in on the wound, but it bled through his fingers. A pool was forming in the ground beside the gravel lane where he had fallen. The pain had subsided, and George knew that he was slipping into shock. His head had that dull feeling one gets with too much cough medicine. His assailant's words came through to him, but the voice seemed far away ... its tone diffused by the oncoming shutdown of his brain. "Ple ... please tell me why you did this. It's about the damned cell phone infrastructure, isn't it?" Geo's own words sounded like hollow echoes.

The man twisted the silencer off of the end of the gun. Putting it into his pocket, he crouched in front of the mortally wounded man. "You've got the gist of it ... it's about the effect, discovered by Dr. F. Guard in the late eighties, when the first crude cell phones were being used." The man added, "It's an effect that may very well be cause for the end of our world. You should know, I don't have anything against you personally

George. But – they pay me pretty handsomely for what I do. Anyway, they discovered a weird thing about a cell phone user's own microwave echoes – what describes the signal that is broadcast out from the phone, usually very close to the user's head, and exactly in step with the words coming from the user's mouth. It was discovered that after many months of using their phones in this way, their brains began to develop the ability to interpret the signals. Directly! The brain is an amazing thing, Mr Dennison."

Geo's eyes were no longer moving. His assailant reached down and felt for a pulse. Standing up, he sighed. "It's too bad you didn't hang around for the best part," he said to no living person. "The way their brains interpret the signals is mostly done subconsciously – in a mode that bypasses what would be filtered or restricted by the conscious mind --- boundaries that would normally be applied --- concepts such as morality. You know Geo, I carry one of the wretched things. Maybe that's what happened to me." Blowing out a breath, he stood up and turned towards the road.

Barry sat on the barstool watching the game. When, thirty minutes later, the hairy fisted one put a fresh, foaming Old Dutch on the bar in front of him, Barry reached instinctively for his wallet. Now the hairy fist moved to Barry's shoulder. "No need for that. Favor from a friend." Barry's mission would go nowhere if he kept drinking. This he knew. But, the first drink seemed to take the edge off of everything. One more wouldn't hurt a thing. "Thanks".

The barkeep smiled, "No problem." By now, the loud crowd

had mostly dispersed – but Barry noted the two strange fellows at the back of the room remained. Seemingly, they had not moved a muscle in two hours. The same demeanor and expression remained on each, as they sat at their separate tables.

By the time the eleven o'clock news started, Barry barely noticed the lead story about the murder of Geo Dennison, top executive of one of the country's leading cell phone companies. Now he was keenly aware of nothing – but cognizant enough to notice his inebriation went beyond the few beers the hairy fist had produced. No – it was not the inebriation of his usual experience. Now he stood away from his barstool, landing his shin smartly up against the next one. He pushed his hands out to steady himself, but a shoulder propped him up. The shoulder was lower than his, and the hands around his waist much smaller. The wispy melodic voice was close in his ears. Barry's head ricocheted off of the frame of the side exit door, but he noticed no pain. Now the lot lights danced on the windshields of the cars in their spaces, and Barry winced at each of them as he passed – trying to focus on the blurry whiteness, wobbling on his feet, moving slowly as two small hands prodded him along.

Now Barry was lying down. He was aware, only dimly, that the side of his face brushed the carpeting of the van floor. Those small hands seemed to be everywhere – vaguely pleasant and soft. The melodic voice came and went, suddenly loud and then soft, ringing in his ears, saying things he could not decipher. There was a flash of light, and then another. Barry reached up to cover his eyes.

The van door opened, and there were rustling sounds as the melodic voice floated away. Now, rough hands hoisted him out into the harsh white light. These hands were not soft, and the voice rough and gritty. Barry was dimly aware that his feet were digging little troughs in the stones, and he was being dragged. Finally, his brain appreciated the fact that he was being roughly treated, and it tried to engage his limbs, to make them fight the gray and black shadows that mishandled him. His head landed on a large stone at the edge of the lot, and this time there was pain.

Barry's face was warm, something he noticed as he awakened. He noticed the wetness - a rough but soft wetness, repeatedly and gently lashing the side of his face. When he opened his eyes, the little terrier was looking down at him. The small dog's smiling face seemed to be saying "what are you doing down here with me?"

The morning sun was mid-sky, and it was hiding behind the tall figure of the man holding the other end of the leash. "Thank the Lord" the elderly black man said. "I was hoping that you'd just tied one on last night, and not something worse." Barry gently pushed the man's little puppy aside, used his arms to push himself to a sitting position, and mumbled "I'm not sure what happened."

"Hey - I know the feeling. I was not always the straight arrow you're looking at." The black man crouched down, saying, "I can buy your coffee over there at the burger stand" as he pointed across the parking lot to the other side of the street.

"Thanks, but I'm OK - I need to get to work." The other man

chuckled, "Sorry about that. Hope you have an understanding boss. Good luck." As the man and his dog walked away, Barry tried to remember the sequence of events that put him on his back in the warm mid-morning sun in an almost empty parking lot. He shook his head, but the cobwebs didn't seem to break loose.

Barry walked across the lot to the only car - his car, and stopped to reach for his keys. "That's odd" he mumbled, as his hand stopped up short in the pocket. The pocket liner had been shorted like a tenderfoot's sheet on the first camp outing. Pushing down hard, he inverted the liner so that he could pull out his keys. He hunched over to insert the car key. It was then that he noticed the over-sized hole in his belt, the hole that had been worn and enlarged because it was the one that made his pants fit best. The prong of the belt was not in that hole. It was two notches away, and his pants dangled loosely on his hips.

A half hour later, Barry entered his apartment. "Where have you been" was the question he expected from Alicia, and she asked it. Her face was more worried than angered. "I'll explain tonight - if I can figure it out."

"Figure it out?"

"Yes. Now I must get to work before I'm fired. Please keep your questions until tonight Alicia. OK?" Alicia nodded, and Barry went through his normal morning routine with as much speed as the pain in his limbs would permit. "You must've really gotten wacked last night. That's not like you."

"Darling, I'll tell you everything I know about it when I get home tonight. OK?" By the time Barry left the apartment, the vague memories and feelings of his night were a little less foggy. He wasn't really sure how much he would tell his wife.

Graham was standing inside the patrolman's entrance to the building for precinct three when Barry came through it. "The captain wants to see you Barry!" Barry knocked, and the captain waved him in. "Please sit down Barry."

"You've broken a very serious rule we have here patrolman Stewart. It's in the code of conduct, and you are supposed to know that by heart. It's the same serious offense even if you don't. Understand?"

Barry started, "I know I'm late, but I think I have an explanation that-" The captain cut him short. "I don't really care how late you are patrolman. You've been prompt - and I could excuse a tardy day. That I could forgive, but you have broken the departments rule about conducting unauthorized investigations, patrolman."

"Mrs. Goodwin came in here. She was in tears, and she wanted to know why we were not keeping her in the loop relative to our investigation into her husband's death. She said that you were leading an investigation into the death, and that (apparently), the police department didn't think it was accidental. Am I correct so far?"

Barry was taken by surprise. His deer in the headlights look did nothing to appease his boss. "I need your gun Barry. I have no choice in this matter. It's a terminate-able offense, and I'm going to have to let you go."

Barry had not even the most nascent of clues about how he might approach the subject of his firing with Alicia. When he entered the apartment, he noticed the note on the counter. "Gone shopping," it said.

Barry found the luger in the nightstand. "Stupid place to put it," he thought, "and an especially stupid place for a police officer to put it." He still thought of himself as one, and not as the ex-officer he had suddenly become. Barry waited four hours for Alicia.

At nine o'clock, he took the luger from the top of the nightstand, and put it into his carry-all bag. It was his father's gun, a war souvenir from his grandfather, and it had been re-machined to take nine millimeter ammunition. Most lugers already took nine millimeter ammo - but this one was special. Its low profile made it easy to hide. It had originally been manufactured as a smaller caliber weapon, but Barry's father had used his machinist skills to modify it. Barry thought about his father, who died during a time that Barry would rather forget. Barry's earliest years saw him as listless and seemingly as the type to go nowhere. A few weeks before his father's death, Barry wrote a letter detailing how much he respected and appreciated his father - for all that he had done - for being there - for being an inspiration. His father died thinking that Barry might not succeed in anything very interesting or important, but knowing that his son held him in high esteem. This Barry was grateful for. Now he pulled the bag over his shoulder, and walked out of the apartment door.

The intersection of Sixth and Jackson streets marked the start of the warehouse district, and that's where she would be. It was a little early for the vice shift, but Barry would find an advantageous spot to take cover. Then he would wait.

Barry's spot in the lower deck stairwell of the dilapidated business gave him a clear shot out onto the street. He sat on the fourth dirty step from the bottom, and peered out between two rusted, half painted wrought iron fence standards. Officer Cindi was easy to spot. She was dressed way over the top -

even by a hooker's standards. She paid little attention to the passing police cruiser that cleared the others from the street. Now the cruiser turned off on Seventh, and Cindi was alone. Barry shoved the luger into the small of her back, saying "Not a word from you Cindi." Cindi knew the feel of a gun in the back, and complied with Barry's directives as he pushed his captive into the parking garage and around the corner of the first opening in a three foot high concrete retainer wall. He shoved her along and down into the lower deck stairwell.

"You drugged me last night. God knows what else you did! What the hell is going on?"

"Let me show you." Cindi reached down into her purse with two fingers. "No gun here Barry. Just my two fingers ... you see ... moving really slow now ... no gun." Now she puckered her lips, "You liked my two fingers Barry, and the other ones as well." Barry heard a hissing sound, like a steam valve going off, and he jerked his head around. Seeing nothing, he jerked his head back around to Cindi, who had pulled her cell phone from her purse. Barry felt faint, and stumbled back against the concrete wall. The stair railing seemed to spin round and round, and the control went out of this legs. He slid down the wall, landing hard, and dropping the gun in front of himself. His brain put out the signal to grab the lost weapon, but the limbs would not respond.

Elliot stood in front of him. "Barry. You're a police officer. Surely you know that the vice chicks always take along a buddy." Elliot was carrying a small plastic gun. It was white in color, and made of some type of plastic or ceramic material. "Neuro toxins, Barry. All the rage in Europe. Not legal here. Some asinine constitutional issue I guess. Some of us have, shall we say, special sources for things. We gotta protect ourselves, you know." Now, Cindi got down on her knees in front of Barry, and held the phone for him to see. "Listen, you little cockroach - this is the reason you will stop trying to screw with us." Cindi pressed a button, and the video began to play. Barry tried to speak, but the words wouldn't come. "Speechless, are you sweetheart? You weren't so speechless last night."

Finally, in broken words Barry sputtered out, "My ... wife ... will believe me ... dirt-bags." Now it was Eliot's turn to speak. "So, you think this is blackmail, you silly son of a bitch? You don't know blackmail like this blackmail buddy boy. We own your ass. Lock, stock, and barrel. This has not a damned thing to do with your wife. This has to do with something else entirely. Cindi - show the man what I mean."

Cindi rewound the video to a particular spot, and showed the screen to Barry. It was readily apparent to Barry that what was showing on the cellphone screen was a stop motion display of the aftermath of the previous night. In the still frame Cindi held out a prophylactic, pinched between two fingers. "See the two fingers, Barry?"

Barry shrugged. His sense of feeling was beginning to return to his limbs. Elliot snorted - "That's all? Just a shrug? From now on, you will do what we say, when we say it, and for as long as we say. You see, there's an unsolved case that you are now associated with Barry. What's that case number Cindi?" Cindi looked down at her phone, then looked up and repeated the number. "It's 123177-AE." Elliot pulled his head back, "Explain to Barry all the implications of case 123177-AE. Why is it so special?"

"Of course Elliot. My pleasure. You see Barry, an eleven year old girl was raped a couple years ago. Her case number was "123177-AE." Seems the case was never solved. Such a sad thing. But - son of a gun - you know - there's some evidence in that girl's rape kit that was never analyzed properly. I'm guessing, that with the right situation, we could get that rape kit re-examined. There would be accusations, a trial, and - you know - it's just so unlikely that the jury could believe that the DNA sample came from my handiwork last night." Cindi pointed to herself, and took a bow. "Nope, not a chance of that my boy!"

Barry wobbled in the direction of the car he had parked far up on Sixth street. The neuro-toxins made him look drunk, and the other ladies he passed along the street noticed that he had good clothes and good shoes. Barry was no bum, by any quick gauge, and a rich drunk always went well on Sixth street. Four blocks from the parking garage he was propositioned by one who was a member of his own precinct. When she recognized him, she smiled and said "I didn't know you were working the street." Just then she tilted her head, cocking it as if she were listening to something. "Oh, I'm so sorry you've been let go. I'm supposed to arrest you now, but that's ridiculous. Soooo ... get lost bucko!" Barry looked around to see if Cindi and her helper were straggling along. "Arrest me for what?"

The young woman laughed, "Waddya think?"

Back at the apartment Alicia was in her favorite spot on the sofa in the corner. She was three quarters through her latest novel, causing Barry to comment when he noticed it. "You're gonna be up late tonight sweetheart, I see." Barry pointed at her book. Alicia shook her head, "No, I normally would finish this thing, since I'm so close to the end. But, it's a lot more important for us to have a talk. What's going on?"

Barry looked like a man permanently lost for words. He moved over to the chair. As he did, his wife's worried eyes followed him. "Let's have this conversation in the morning Alicia." Alicia shook her head, "No way. Your dresser drawer was left open and your luger was gone. When you came home I noticed that you didn't have your service weapon. Did you get fired? And what are you doing with the luger?"

Barry released all of his breath, in a resigned, but exasperated sort of way. He slumped over, putting his elbows onto his knees. It's insane Licia. Completely insane. He began to unwind the story, telling her about the bar and the drugging. Then he stopped, and looked at her. Nope, he couldn't tell her. Suddenly he understood her personal pain more clearly. It wasn't always a thing only about oneself.

"I'm doing nothing with the luger ... don't worry. As far as my job goes, I'll tell you in the morning." Alicia's look was a combination of displeasure and concern. "Alright," she said with disappointment. "I'll wait."

Barry slept till nine, and that was enough to clue Alicia in on at least part of the unexplained story. 9:05 brought a heavy banging at the door, and Barry bolted upright in his bed. "What's the problem?" he blurted out, as he rolled off the mattress and pulled his clothing from the chair where he had tossed it. Barefoot, he opened the door. "Graham," Barry exclaimed. "What is going on?" Graham nodded, "Courier work for the latest newbie sex netter. You."

"I'm not a sex netter." Graham shook his head, "Now you are."

Barry started to close the door, but Graham pushed it open. By this time Alicia had rounded the corner in her robe. Seeing the uniformed police officer, she asked "What's the problem officer?" Graham smiled, "Your lucky husband found something else to do, since they gave him a little vacation from the force. Probably permanent, fraid to say. But, we have some other work to - you know - put some bread and butter on the table. I'm sure you'll appreciate that Mrs. Stewart." Barry's eyes met Graham's patronizing drivel with scorn. "Why the frown honey? They've got something else for you to do."

"I'm thinking about some other options, that's all, Alicia." Graham laughed, saying "Barry, you know this is your best option," as he pulled a large, rolled, manila envelope from his back pocket. He moved closer to Barry, and pulled back the seal. "Remember these *documents* we went over last night?"

Barry's face paled. "You!" Barry cut himself short. He vaguely remembered the flash of light in the van. "Fine," finally came from his lips. "I'll do this courier business. Today. Nothing promised for later."

When the twosome reached the lot outside of the apartment, Barry saw that Graham was driving an unmarked vehicle. "Get in. Our first stop is J.R. Benlivo's place."

Barry was incredulous, "Excuse me?" "Yes, the cell phone company president Barry. That one. We walk in prominent circles my boy."

The car was waved through the private gate at the entrance to the community. "You know, J.R. and his company are coming on strong. Right on the heels of Sky Tiger they say. Twenty eight percent market penetration. Good business. Good for us." Barry's face assumed a look that had become routine for him and his countenance - a blank one, one clearly not decoding any messages.

"Barry, do you think you're the only one? What do you think those nice ladies are doing down on South Sixth? Any ideas?"

Barry's scornful look returned, "Wasting the precinct's money, I take it."

"Nah - not at all. We arrest the poor ones. But guys like J.R., they're just like you Barry ... just like you. You should feel a real kinship. By golly, you're going to meet the man today, you lucky dog."

The mansion was impressive, by any standard Barry was familiar with. They rounded the long drive, and pulled to a stop under the decorative canopy port. "Just go to the door Barry, and tell them you're from bank security. J.R. will give you something. Bring it back. You'll eventually do this all by yourself. Then, maybe you two can share war stories. Today though, I think he is in a hurry. Something tells me."

Barry again looked incredulous. "You're blackmailing this man? J.R. just gave five million dollars to the Redemption Army, and I hear he gives just as generously to his church. He sure as hell doesn't seem like the type, if you ask me. I mean, morality is not exactly equivalent to sexual mores, however - the South Street boys strike me as way more narcissistic."

"That's why I said you're like J.R. Both of you were hooked up by other means. You know how it was with yourself. J.R. was the same but different. His undoing was having sex with his wife."

"So, you subverted the poor man's wife. Good gaw-"

"No. Nothing like that. He was a laundry hamper job. That's mostly how we bring in the goodie two shoes."

"Laundry hamper?"

"He and his old lady love each other. Such a lucky fellow. So, our surveillance boys know when they - you know - love each other. That's all it takes. He's rich, so he hires Terrible Maids, Inc. That's us. Pretty neat, huh?"

"And if they're not rich enough for a maid?"

Graham shook his head, "Do I have to explain everything? That's why our boys in the legislature created the concept of deputized citizens doing legal *walk-throughs*, unknown by and in the absence of the homeowner. You know about that, right?"

"So you blackmailed everybody in our legislature?"

Graham laughed, "Same way, my man - it works for all classes of customer. I see J.R. at the door. Go get it tenderfoot!"

Barry retrieved the package. It was a nondescript box with the tabs folded into a lock. He tossed the package onto the seat, but he did not get back into the car. "That's dirt money, isn't it?"

"It's more than you have in your wallet. The first three bills are yours just for doing such a bang up job."

"You can keep your money Graham. I'm no criminal. You'll shoot me in the back or you won't - but screw you - I'm not interested."

Barry slammed the door hard shut, and then started walking away from the car and across the long lawn towards the road ...

4

Documents

B arry knew something was wrong before he entered the apartment. The door was hanging open, and there were boxes and papers strewn in the entryway. As his heart jumped into his throat, he raced around - going frantically from room to room, looking for his wife. Barry didn't find her, but he noticed that her favorite things were missing. Missing was the the little statuette of the cat and the old woman - a ceramic equivalent of the stereotypical Rockwell scene. Missing were their two biggest pieces of luggage and many of the better things in her wardrobe, which was hanging open. She had *left him* in a hurry.

Barry walked into the kitchen. Duplicates of the *documents* that Graham had shown him were pasted onto the refrigerator, pinned there by two Acme Appliance magnets. In large lipsticked letters, it read "This hurts me more than two years ago!"

Barry folded down onto the barstool next to the counter. He put his head down and let his less manly emotions run their course. Twenty minutes later, he picked up the phone and dialed the one person he any longer trusted in this world: his mother.

As Barry hung up the phone, he realized that he had the same problem with his mother as he had with Alicia. His situation was too bizarre to explain to anyone, and now he knew that even a close friend or relative would be more likely to attribute his words to temporary craziness, too much stress, or other things equally removed from the truth. He walked around in the little apartment, looking around in disbelief. A couple times he pulled on his hair till it hurt - hoping it was all just a real bad dream. He half-heartedly began a clean-up of all that was strewn by Alicia's hurried, furious exit. He went to bed early, hoping for a temporary respite from the nightmare, but sleep would not come until mid morning. He was back up at six, unrested and feeling no better.

By nine he was at the ATM machine, cursing. Their joint account never had much in it at any time during the month, but he had just been paid. While riding the three blocks to the bank on the corner, he realized the likelihood that anything was left. "That's alright," he told himself, "... she needs it more than I."

Back at the apartment, he took inventory. He counted four cans of pork 'n beans, two plates of leftover enchiladas, a bag of cookies, and not much else.

Somehow, Barry managed to get through the rest of the week on the pitiful shelf bottoms of the pantry. He realized that on Monday - he would have to try to find some work.

He sat on the floor of his apartment, jotting notes into his notebook, and circling various advertisements in the papers he had spread out on the floor. B & N Security, A-1 Security Corps, and Rent-A-Guard seemed most promising. It would be quicker to find work for one of these places than it would be to find law enforcement work - even without the blot on his resume.

By Tuesday morning, he had successfully arranged for an

interview with one of the agencies.

The receptionist at A1 pointed at a chair in the lobby. "He's running a little behind schedule" she said. Barry took the chair, and picked up a copy of *Security Weekly*. The woman in the corner was fussing with her kid - maybe all of four years old. Barry found himself thinking that it might not be such a great way to do an interview, but maybe she had no other choice. Glancing at her out of the corner of his eye, he decided that she was a little small for security work, other than maybe working the guard shack at some company.

Barry had become engrossed by an article in the magazine, so he wasn't very sure he had heard it. It seemed improbable, he thought, that the kid could have said something like that. He glanced over at the child, and noticed that her mother was giggling. As Barry looked at her, she became embarrassed, and so Barry went back to his magazine. Suddenly the little kid repeated the words, this time saying them loudly. "That's the sex predator who tries to be a cop!" Barry was embarrassed and infuriated at the same time. "What the hell?" Had the kid really said that? He couldn't say he hadn't heard it, but it was one of the most surreal things Barry had ever experienced. Now the mother looked at him in an accusatory fashion. She was still smiling, but in a condescending sort of way, and Barry felt the flush of anger take him again. "Your kid says some strange things, maam" was about all he could muster. The embarrassment was weird because - well - Barry knew he was perfectly innocent. It was more about the fact that the woman and her kid had information - false information, containing within it a smear that was incredibly nasty and that any random stranger shouldn't possess. To make it worse, it had been delivered by a four year old kid.

The woman walked to the receptionist's counter. Barry could

hear some explanation about her kid being sick, forcing her to cancel the appointment. As she pushed the door open under the exit sign at *A1 Security*, the woman turned back to look at Barry. Shaking her head slowly, she delivered one of the most hostile looks Barry had ever received from a woman. Finally she was gone, leaving Barry to contemplate the day's most bizarre event, tacked onto the most bizarre week of his life.

J.F. Smythe was lettered on the door. The receptionist saw Barry hesitate at the door, and she waved at him. "Just walk on in. He asked for you."

"Have a seat," said J.F.

"I must apologize for my schedule running late. We've had a pretty strong day for recruits. Good thing, I guess."

Barry thought it might not be such a good thing, since it would mean more competition. "It says on your resume that you have a law enforcement related degree - forensics - and that you've done a stint with the local police. Only two months indicated. Is that a mistake? "

Barry looked down, and J.F. interjected, "Ah - well it didn't work out? May I ask why?"

"Personality conflict." Barry flushed again. What was he to say? Now he was thinking that he should have left the police work off of his resume. It was too late for that, because the damage already registered on the interviewer's face.

"Listen, you look like a great guy. Personality conflicts do happen. Do you own a sidearm?"

"Sort of. I've temporarily lost custody of it. I should be able to rectify that in a week or so. I was hoping that wouldn't be a problem."

J.F. shook his head. "No, the position we need you for requires a gun, and it starts tomorrow. Sorry for that. Maybe you can check back with us when you've located your gun. Well - that's all I have for you now. Good luck." Barry shook J.F's hand and turned to walk to the door. Just as his hand touched the door handle, J.F. added, "You need to find that luger. Those antiques are worth money you know!"

Barry nodded and walked out. He walked past the receptionist's desk and stopped short. Finally, it hit him. He was furious. How could this man know about his luger? It was unregistered, having been given to him before mandatory registration rules. It was an antique, which provided him with additional privacy. The gun was absolutely secret. Only his mother, wife, and now, unfortunately - Elliot and his associates, could possibly know about it.

Barry jumped into his car and pulled out onto the Boulevard. Noon traffic was picking up, and the lights were long. A noisy Harley rider rode his bike up into the lane next to Barry. The biker's girlfriend kept throwing looks Barry's way. It occurred to Barry that she was giving him some kind of come-on. She puckered her lips to blow him a kiss. Now the bearded rider on the seat in front of her twisted his head, "She's not for you - sex predator!" The grisly looking man gunned the cycle's engine, jamming the loud cackle of the exhaust into Barry's ear.

By Friday, Barry had wasted time on two more interviews. Neither of them proved to be worthwhile, even though Barry dropped the detail about the stint at "precinct three" from the pages of his resume.

Barry was thinking about calling his mother. He hated the idea of giving her a money call. He didn't call her enough as it was, and he didn't want one of those rare occasions when he *did call her* to be for money. But, the pantry was empty. No choice. He put his hand down onto the phone, but was stopped by a loud banging noise made by his front door knocker. He walked across the kitchen, then across the small living room and entryway, and he opened the door.

Before the door was fully open, Barry already recognized the blue and yellow plaid miniskirt, and those legs that the owner seemed to be so darned proud of.

"It's you. No thanks." Barry started to close the door. Cindi moved forward and shoved her hand through the door opening. She held the luger tightly around its barrel, shoving the handle end towards Barry.

Barry was caught off guard and backed away from the door. Cindi stood in the entryway, and before Barry could say another word, her hand pressed over his mouth. Her left hand muffled Barry's "What the fu-" just as he noticed the note she held in her right one: "Don't say anything!" He looked down at the luger that Cindi had shoved, handle first, into his grasp. Barry repeated the *WTF,* but this time only in his head.

Cindi handed Barry a half sheet of notebook paper upon which she had written a few lines. He read through the lines, and handed the page back to its owner. The ex-policeman's facial expression morphed into something else. Belligerent anger had changed to true, blank, non-comprehension. Barry couldn't believe that he was doing it, but he followed Cindi's shapely form out to her car, and got into it, using the passenger side door. After she pulled away from the little street that ran to the *cul-de-sac* where he and Alicia had lived, he started to speak. "No!" shouted Cindi as she pressed the accelerator and sped out onto the boulevard.

They passed the city limit sign, and she pressed the accelerator harder, going ten miles over - then twenty. "It's OK, I'm a police officer" she said with a grin. As Barry again began to speak, she put her finger to her lips.

She turned onto a side road, and down along a long row of self storage units. About half the distance to the end, she pressed the brake and stopped the car. The lot was devoid of other people or vehicles. She walked around to the rear of the car, and then over to one of the units. It was nondescript and indistinguishable from the others, excepting for a small metal tag with the number "1956" burnished onto it, and riveted into the door next to the lock. Cindi pulled a key from her purse and inserted it into the lock. She was about to reach for the door handle, but Barry beat her to it, pulling up on it until the miniature garage door was fully retracted into the bay.

The bay was nearly empty excepting for the little gasoline engine powered cycle standing up on its kickstand in the center of the space. The thing was too tiny to be a motorcycle, but larger than the typical moped.

Cindi ignored both the cycle and Barry, and trotted to the rear of the space, and to a small metal crate resting on the floor. Another lock on the crate required another key, which Cindi quickly produced from the underside of the seat on the moped. Inserting the key and twisting it, she threw open the metal lid of the crate, and extracted a small rectangular box - an aluminum box that Barry guessed was eight inches long and almost, but not quite square. At the top of the box Barry could see a coil of metal that reminded him vaguely of a stove-top element.

Now Cindi extracted an automotive battery from the crate, and the muscles on her trim arms bulged slightly as she pulled it up and out of the container, and then carried it over to the cycle, where she deposited it into a basket carrier welded onto the side of it. Back to the crate she went, producing yet another battery, which she placed on the other side of the cycle inside of a similarly welded support.

Barry could contain himself no more, and started laughing. Cindi jumped up, pointing at him and frantically shaking her head. Just under her breath, she hissed out the word "No!" Barry's face resumed its blank look of non-comprehension. Cindi took two cables from the crate, and attached each one to the little box. She attached the other ends of the cables to large bolted clips attached to the batteries on each side of the cycle. She deposited the little box into a saddlebag on the back of the cycle. Now Cindi pushed the bike out onto the stones, put the kickstand down, walked back to the door, and closed it. She pointed at Barry and mouthed the word "Stay." She got into the car, drove it down to the end of the storage lot, over a small bridge, and up into an empty church parking lot. Barry could see her small form walking back, retracing the movement of the car, but in reverse.

Five minutes later, Cindi strode up to the bike, throwing her leg across the seat of it, and pointing to a spot on the seat behind her. Barry looked around. It was obvious, Barry thought, that little Cindi was crazy. However; it would be a hell of a long walk back to town. He slid behind her onto the seat of the bike.

When she cleared the stones of the drive, and had straightened the cycle out so that it ran straight along the small two lane road, she said, "Now you can talk all you want."

"You're crazy" were Barry's first words.

"Ya think? Tell me about your life lately. I'll give you some time."

Barry said nothing, and the cycle droned out it laborious sound, complaining that it wasn't built for the load that it was being asked to haul.

Cindi turned her head while talking to the bike, saying "C'mon Betsy." She turned her head further, shouting back to Barry, "It's a Peugeot. 1978. Damned good year for mopeds. No electronics, no unnecessary garbage attached to it.   Just moped. It was built before the law governored the maximum speed for unlicensed mopeds - it'll do fifty - easy, with me on it, but you're bogging us down a little."

Barry noticed the speedo was stuck at thirty five, and it seemed that Cindi's wrist had twisted the throttle as far as it would go.

Now they were going downhill, and Betsy stopped complaining. The speedo ticked up. The state park sign flew by, and then another that contained the words "Natural Preserve Area. Dangerous animals may be present. Hike in this area at your own risk. "

Cindi pulled up next to an old shelter house. It was obviously in a state of neglect and disrepair, and tall weeds grew up around the place. Cindi shook her hand, indicating that Barry should dismount the cycle. She jumped off of it, and kicked down the stand. She had parked the bike a few feet from one of the dilapidated picnic benches in the shelter. She hopped up on the top of the table closest to the bike. She turned to Barry, saying "The out of state visitors never go past that sign you saw back there. Works nicely for people who need to be alone. Like us."

"Let me get this straight. You doped me, raped me, destroyed my career, hooked me up with ruthless criminals, ginnied up bogus evidence - thanks to my drugged rape - in order to have me imprisoned for the rest of my natural life, and topped it off by destroying my marriage. Now, you think we need some quality *alone* time."

Cindi reached into the saddlebag on the bike, and pulled her purse out of it. She took three hundred dollars in large bills, and handed them to Barry.

Barry held his head back, "Huh?" "It's OK now if you pay me? I don't want your hookering money, and it's definitely not OK!"

"This is not hooker money. I'm not a hooker. I didn't rape you."

Barry's blank look returned. "You're crazy. You need help."

"The world is crazy Barry. Literally. You need a little remedial history lesson, since they didn't see fit to give you the accurate one in school. That's why I brought you out to this little park where the state's sign says we could be eaten by bears ... and ... also ... because I know I can trust you now."

"Trust me? You figure you can trust guys you've raped?"

"I told you ... I didn't rape you. It was faked ... all faked. You don't need to worry about the case number that Eliot is so proud of. The stuff they put in the kit came from my kitchen Barry. I've done this quite a few times. I try to save the good ones, like you Barry. The world is in the midst of a takeover by do-badders. Real b-hole level do-badders. Only a few conceive this now, and fewer seem to have the balls to stand up to it. There are not many guys like you Barry. You told them to go to hell, even with sure long-term prison time as a consequence." "Balls."

"I take it you didn't major in English."

"I say do-badders Barry, as opposed to do-gooders. Do you know who the do-gooders are? They are those millions who are eternally unaware that they are being manipulated to do evil. The real rotten apples are, as we speak, tightening their hold on every facet of human existence. Every port of power is being infiltrated. They maintain a sprinkling of do-gooders as a smoke screen, and manipulate them so that - most of the time – they and millions like them fail to realize they are doing the bidding of the manipulators. Evil. Evil Barry, like this world has never seen."

Barry's look changed a little. Maybe, he thought, Cindi wasn't bad, and instead just sheer off the planet crazy. He managed to bring up half a smile, saying, "Seems to me that we could have had this conversation in a coffee shop."

Cindi shook her head and pointed to her cycle. "Didn't my daddy's contraption raise your curiosity level?"

"My curiosity has been on a leave of absence lately - *without pay*."

Cindi laughed, "See, you still have your sense of humor. You're gonna need it Bubalouie. Big time." Then she continued, "My dad was always a tinkerer. He built things - electronics and whatnot - as a sort of hobby. When I was a kid, he always seemed to have a soldering iron in his hand. He was always telling me to stay away so I wouldn't get burned. I'm really jumping ahead in my story. You're gonna be confused unless I backtrack a little."

"I started out with the police department five years ago. I don't have college - not any - and so they gave me a meter maid job. Can you believe? I was a freak'in meter maid. Well, the honchos there realized that guys find me attractive. Well, all except you, apparently. So, after a year they bumped me over to vice. My life was forever changed, but not in a good way, because I managed to learn about things that I wish I hadn't.

Anyway, I found out that the system is stinking corrupt - top to bottom. It is just absolutely stinking to high heaven corrupt. Everybody is on the take. Everybody is doing bad. I haven't found many like you Barry. Not very G-damned many. It's too bad, cause it's making it easy for them."

Little Cindi took a breath. It was obvious to Barry that she had the weight of the world on her shoulders. "Pretty damned tough little woman," he thought to himself.

"When I switched over to vice, they said that I was in a department that required high security. They said that it was dangerous work, and that I needed to have a procedure done, in order to *protect me* from all of those vile, rutting ogres roaming the streets looking for little ol' me."

They said it would hurt only a little bit. Lying bastards. It hurt a hell of a lot. They put a little chip in the back of my ear canal. The *precinct three* doctors did this, and they used some sort of air powered gun. It's buried in there about three eighth's of an inch, and it would be a bloody mess to get it back out. I hate the thing. I went to a doctor to have it removed. He recognized it right away and refused to take it out."

"What's it for?"

"Well, originally they gave me the story that it was basically nothing more than a fancy bluetooth earpiece that could work with my cell phone. It does work with my cell phone - the same way as my old bluetooth earpiece. What they didn't tell me, is that the damned thing can be used to track me wherever I go.

Bastards. But that's not all. It can monitor whatever I say, anywhere, anytime. This they didn't tell me. I found out another way.

I was engaged to be married about the time I joined vice and got this thing shot into my head. The guys at the station kept repeating things back to me that I had said to my fiancée. In bed! It was driving me nuts, so I started taking the battery out of my cell phone. It didn't help! It was surreal for me. Surreal - big word for a no-college girl, eh? I decided it was the damned security chip. It was the only thing that made sense. Over the next couple years, I learned more and more about the ways this world of ours is being turned into a fascist hell. You know, some of those johns I was supposed to arrest? I took them to bed. Call me a whore, but this is a war in my opinion ... it's just getting started ... nobody knows yet. Well, nobody except the nasty ogre b-holes and a few like us. Only a very few like us, Barry. Anyway, I gave up my virtue for a couple guys I thought might be in the know - people who basically run the security business, and people who run the companies that make these damned things." Cindi pointed to her ear. "They basically confirmed what I thought, in so many words. Damn them!"

Cindi pointed at the cycle. "That's where my old man comes in. I managed to socially engineer the inner ear-ring frequency range from one of the guys I bedded. That's what they call these things - inner ear-rings. Cute, eh? So ... then I made up some story for my dad, saying that the department needed a jammer for the inner ear-ring frequency range, and I asked if he could make one. I'm pretty sure he thought I was crazy, but he did it anyway. He took it as a challenge, and he could never say no to his little girl. His gizmo kills off everything so long as I'm within about ten feet. The nice thing is - if I take it with me on the cycle - they can't track me. So, now you know why we didn't go to a coffee shop."

Barry nodded, "So, why not use your car?"

"My car!? Bugged to high heaven! If they can put a chip in my ear that does all the shit it does, and it's the size of a split pea, then how in the freak'in hell would I ever find one that they put on my car? Think man! Think!"

Barry took offense. "You're a little condescending there-" Cindi jumped up off of the table, and walked up to Barry, putting her face about six inches from his, saying "Sorry. But, part of the problem is that people are in future shock about technology. They simply don't work this shit into their logical thought processes because they haven't caught up with this hurtling death ball of technology, rolling downhill, getting bigger and bigger, spiraling out of control. The ones who do consciously comprehend it see it as overpowering and just give in. Give up. That's what we're up against. You do know that pea-sized full blown cell phones were available for embedding in industrial equipment ten years ago already? The reality is that this shit is here, it's being used in nefarious - terrible - ways, and people refuse to so much as think about it. They blow it out of their minds, using the twenty year old reason that "the crazies talk implants." That twenty year old reason is no longer valid ... at all. But, our brains won't keep pace with technology. If you were an evil ass shit, would you pass up on this kind of thing? Hell no! Believe me, they aren't."

Cindi realized she was spitting in Barry's face, and backed away. "Sorry. This shit gets me going. Why do you think that they bury these things in our flesh? Why not just give us a damned bluetooth ear-piece? It's simple. They know we'll figure out that we're being tracked like dogs with these things, and if they were not buried in our heads, we'd just toss them away. Or not take them with us. Of course. It's not about making sure we are safe! No! It's about always knowing where we are and what we are doing so that they can control us! So that we can't stop them!

Barry walked over to the bench, and sat down next to Cindi. He turned to her and said, "So, who is behind this?"

"Boy, did you ever open up a can of worms there Bubalouie! I've been sleeping all over the place trying to find out. I've formulated all kinds of theories over the past couple years, but one seems to be more fleshed out with bits of pillow talk than the others."

Barry looked at Cindi. She was, by any man's standard, gorgeous. What was coming out of her mouth was anything but what would be expected. She had lowered herself into a rotten barrel of sewage in order to fight a war for what was intrinsic to her soul and her being. The essence of her spirit was to detest corruption and the rule of evil men, and was willing to do almost anything to fight against those things.

"So, you think I'm a lesser person now - because I've done what I've done - with these men?"

"No."

"So, what do you think?"

"I don't know."

"So, you think I'm crazy?"

Now the first real smile came to Barry's lips. He couldn't believe that he was starting to like her. She had ... what's the word? Intensity? Spunk? He wasn't sure. Cindi had caused him one hell of a lot of trouble. As his memory flashed back to the picture on the refrigerator, he realized that his marriage was probably permanently wacked. "My brain is a mess of unconnected things right now Cindi. You've caused a great deal of turmoil to happen in my life. But, I believe you thought you were helping me by doing what you did. I had a thought that, assuming I could find her, you could say to Alicia what you just said to me, and she'd come back. But, you know, she'd just call the two of us the same thing. Nuts. Your story is nuts. Maybe the world is nuts. Maybe I'm nuts. Some of what you say matches what has happened to me in the past week. So, if they straight jacket you, they may decide to do me too. Guess I won't call 'em out."

Barry scanned Cindi's petite form from top to bottom. It was one of those things that some guys do automatically, almost unconsciously. He tried to stop the reflex of his eyes, but it was too late.

"You know I've seen that look a few times Bubalouie." Barry smiled again. "You know, if we were two rabbits, and I were daydreaming this scene, we'd be hopping each other's bones right now. I mean, you come to me half dressed, take me on a bad, bad motor scooter ride into the forest, and tell me crazy stories. Every schoolboy's dream."

Cindi flushed, and Barry couldn't believe it. Not as tough a little chickadee as you seem, he thought. He walked further into the little shelter, and twisted around on one foot. Looking down, he said, "I'm Sorry. I really love my wife, you know. I won't admit to this little daydream. Not ever."

Cindi looked a little disappointed. Barry came back to her, and again he sat next to her on the bench. "So ... about this history lesson I'm missing?"

"One of the guys was a real high roller ... department of

defense guy maybe ... defense contractor maybe ... he wouldn't say, even drunk."

"He was just totally dejected. I mean, it was like he fought a war and was on the losing side. I kept pouring, and he kept talking. It seemed he could keep the secret parameters, even in his stupor, but I got a general idea about what he was saying. At first, I thought he was crazier than drunk. I'm still not sure about it."

"What did he say?"

"He said that there is a Triumvirate."

"A what?"

"A Triumvirate. Three main powers. Basically, the three are the Communist Republic of China, Europe, including the Soviet Union, and the United States."

"I think maybe you're the one who missed the history lesson. There is no Soviet Union. Secondly, you have basically described the entire developed world."

"About the developed world - you are precisely correct. About the demise of the Soviet Union - you are incorrect. At least, that's what the man said. What made him drink was not the existence of this Triumvirate that he talked about. It was that our country doesn't control anything, and the Triumvirate controls everything. Completely. He said we are no longer a sovereign nation, and that the Triumvirate now controls the world."

Barry looked at Cindi blankly. Then he shook his head up and down, in the manner of someone who doesn't really believe, but knows that the conversation must go on, and will, belief or no belief.

"He said the fall of the U.S.S.R. was faked."

"So, they fake everything these days - rape - and iron curtain falls. Amazing."

"Listen Bubalouie. His words, not mine."

"He said they came up with a super spy device that takes advantage of a hidden portion of electromagnetic theory, a portion of the theory that was concealed by several very smart people who lived at the beginning of our understanding of electrical phenomenon. He said the group included Einstein. These people had pretty much a politically powered hold on scholarly thought, and they formed the equations and theories that were used exclusively up until the Soviet's rediscovery of the hidden portion."

"So, if this is known, our people could use the same equations, and develop a so-called super spy device."

"Apparently, there was some catch twenty-two problem that the Soviets figured out long before us. They used the time during which they had exclusive control of the technology in order to take control of most of the developed world's governments. They faked the fall of the Soviet Union because they knew they could take control of the world with the device they developed. Again, his words, not mine."

"Think about it Barry. Has an authoritarian dictatorship ever voluntarily given up power, in any century of our planet's history? Nah - it's a silly idea, but the rest of the world swallowed it, hook, line, and sinker. So he said."

"He said most spy devices work on the principle of beams ... radio beams ... radar beams ... sonar beams ... laser optical beams, etcetera. He said that the new technology relies on fields instead of beams to spy on things. He said it is like a giant MRI machine, with the whole world inside of it, allowing them to spy on any part of the planet they wish. He said that their computers could project any geographical point on earth in infinite detail – that they could, in virtual fashion, be in any room in any house, church, school, or government building. They could sit and listen to any conversation held anywhere, anyplace. The Soviet's own word for this thing is "The God Machine."

"Do you believe any of this?"

Barry looked reflective. "I don't know. You sure remember it all in fine detail."

"The guy was drunk, and I was not. He was talking very slowly, and kept repeating himself. Believe me, I remember it all pretty well."

"So he said that the Soviets didn't say anything for quite a while. They spent years collecting dirt on every senator, congressman, congresswoman, corporate exec, and every other high roller or mover-shaker sort of person. One day, they dropped the other foot, committing a total blackmail, across the board, of our government and most of the others in the Western world. It was like your ginnied up DNA case, except it was at the nation level instead of at the local level. Our local corruption is driven by this. When the top end is corrupt, then everything below it will be also. Some things trickle downhill, but corruption flows like a tide. Corrupt politicians hire only corrupt contractors. It goes like a pandemic – like a plague.

Anyway, he said that our government realized they had been strategically compromised. Every plan, the location of every nuke, the codes for everything - the Soviets had been able to find. The drunk man didn't say anything for a long while. I thought his drunken stupor had finally killed the conversation. Then he said, "We almost pushed the button. We knew the consequences of capitulation to the Soviets, and that there would be no way to backtrack from it. They'd basically take over everything. It was crazy insane nihilistic, but we told them we were going to push the button, and they believed us." They called everyone to the table, and that was the genesis for the Triumvirate. A shared global power, which stripped individual nations of their constitutions, became the real power over every country - and over ignorant populaces, for the most part unaware of the takeover.

The Triumvirate has no real constitution - it's just an authoritarian regime. Of course it is. The blackmailed nations have representatives who are are pretty much rubber stampers for the main leaders, who come from the Soviet Union, China, and a couple from Europe. We have nobody with any clout, really."

"So, the drunk guy said some other things. Our defense people tried to fight back. They built a giant field generator in Alaska. They put it up there thinking the Triumvirate wouldn't notice. Somehow our people got away with building it, and then turned it on. It works by blasting huge amounts of power up into the ionosphere, which is reflected down and somehow, apparently, washes out the field aberrations that let the spy system work. He guessed it's marginally effective. The Triumvirate destroyed a dozen or so of our top government people in retaliation, but I think he said that the machine is still running."

"All kinds of crap goes on behind the scenes, over a blithely ignorant populace, because our government people are forced to rubber stamp everything. Second level spycraft is being put everywhere, on orders from the Triumvirate. The Chinese have been ordered to put back-door spy access capability into all consumer electronic equipment, even including music players. Everything! Now it takes only a thumb-drive with some simple interface electronics to scan any laptop or music player. All the manufacturers have been ordered to participate.

Go to a coffee shop - anywhere - and have your screen and keystrokes pulled off by a low level Triumvirate spy - people who, by the way, are everywhere."

"It's all working together, Barry. The clowns I work with - the Eliots and the Grahams - they are all manipulated by low level cruds with Triumvirate allegiances. They took over the government with their fancy spy machine, the *God Machine*, and they're taking control of the streets with the likes of Eliot and Graham. It's all about control - absolute, brutal, authoritarian control. It's about a noose so tight that the Triumvirate can never be unseated. Permanent tyranny."

Cindi stopped talking. Neither said anything for a long time. Finally, Barry volunteered, "You've given me an interesting story told to you by a drunk man."

"So, you don't believe it?"

"I don't know. But, I will say that I think I've been followed lately. Random people on the street tell me I'm a sex predator."

"It's your cell phone Bubalouie."

"My cell phone? If it were my cell phone, then we'd have been tracked here ... in which case, all of your Daddy's soldering skills just went down the drain."

"Where is your cell phone Barry?"

"It's right here, on my belt clip." Barry reached down and flipped the flap on the little leather belt carrier. Now he looked down to see that it was empty.

"Looking for this?"

Barry glanced up to see Cindi, who had his cell phone in one hand and its battery in another. "How'd you do that?"

"I used to play pick-pocket with my classmates when I was a kid. I'm pretty good I think. Maybe a second career there ... "

Barry laughed.

"About the battery ... you see Barry, they might let a tenderfoot go for *breaching the trust*, as the Triumvirate lackeys like to say. But I'm not sure what would happen to me. Of course, there's the rumor about Jere."

"You know what happened to Jere?"

"Well, I overheard part of a conversation Graham and Eliot were having one day. I definitely heard the name Jere mentioned, and a little later, something that seemed to be about a person being *put down*. I think they know at least a little bit about what happened to Jere. Graham and Eliot were never in the good guy crowd, to say the least, but they were once a hell of a lot better than they are now. It's the same with some of the other guys."

"Corruption killing off the soul?"

"Yeah - that may be part of it. But ... I don't know ... I think it has really been downhill since they took the implants. They both came into vice after me, so I saw them degenerate. Sounds crazy, doesn't it?"

"Cindi, you've not said a single thing that isn't crazy. I'm not saying that I don't believe you, or at least believe that you believe you. I do have some things in my recent past to keep my finger off of the 911 speed-dial, assuming you were to give the phone back to me." Cindi handed the phone to Barry. "If you put the battery in, I'll shoot you." Barry thought he saw a smile, but the young woman's eyes were profoundly serious. "No problem."

The ride back to the self serve storage facility was quiet. They stopped in the church parking lot first, and Cindi asked Barry to pack the moped away. "One of these days, they'll wonder why I'm spending so much time in church." Barry looked at her, "Should be obvious."

Cindi and Barry met a few times over the coming weeks, and Barry always remembered to kill his cell phone. When he was by himself, he kept it on, hoping against probable futile odds for a call from Alicia. He had tried her number to no avail, and came to the conclusion that she had ditched her old phone. Her mother refused to talk to him.

Barry began to pick up more and more on the innuendos of random passer-bys - stuff seemingly directed at him, wherever he went. Yes, they were using the phone to track him. It was a certainty. "There's the sex predator who tried to be a cop" seemed to be a favorite, but other nastiness was blended into the mix. Perplexing to Barry was the randomness. They were presumably strangers, otherwise going about their normal days. It was like the cell phone system had been usurped by a computer colossus, capable of finding strangers close enough to berate him, and sending the commands to do so.

Barry began to notice people walking around muttering derogatory things about those gathered around them. Venom was directed not only at him, but others too. Some of them literally never stopped talking. They were like walking, talking little machines, never saying anything from their own minds, but instead repeating the mantras and directed insults that originated from their cell phones. They were little propaganda machines, repeating twisted words that indeed carried tangential connections to him, but that were stripped of real truth. This new order possessed a propaganda machine surely good to make the emperor green with envy. Tokyo Rose, Triumvirate version. Had the people really given up their own thought processes to the machine? Of course it was them, in their masses, that the colossus sought to control – and not him. He was only the bait, set by the machine, and needed to make it work. The seeds of resistance that might otherwise appear on the fields of the *proletariat,* now could be crushed simply by manipulating the masses against themselves. On Triumvirate command, they would seek out and crush the seed under their own feet. Armies had become superfluous.

On the next meeting with Cindi, Barry mentioned his theory. "Normal people wouldn't do this." Cindi shook her head. "I think that the Triumvirate no longer fears the little unsovereign governments that it controls. They see the only possible resistance as coming from what you just called the *proletariat.*"

"They take advantage of the biggest weakness of the proletariat in order to control them - the *Dudley-do-right* urge. The Triumvirate manipulates the little people with this. They track them with their cell phones, and me with with my implant. The Dudley's are not important enough to receive implants, and could revolt against that. So, the triumvirate uses phones for the same effect. Some huge portion of the populace recites shit on command, doing the will of the Triumvirate. It's a tyrant's dream."

"Barry, I think the Triumvirate controls the school systems to entrain students *not* to think, and to be the little puppets you mentioned. The new order wants this. They want a proletariat too dumb to avoid the shackles of the Triumvirate."

5

Betsy

B arry sat at the kitchen counter. The refrigerator door was clean, the pieces of his problem were likely several miles downstream by now. He picked up his cellphone. He surfed to a popular news press site, and posted a lament to the comments section. The comments to his comment were mostly supportive, and it was nice to unload things anonymously. He put the phone in his clip and went to bed.

Barry hadn't bothered to set the alarm, and it was nearly noon when he rolled out of bed. He tossed a couple week old bread end-crusts into the toaster and shoved the lever down. Cindi was keeping his stomach from growling too much, but he didn't like taking the money from her. Its source, he reasoned, would almost certainly make him feel squeamish. Sitting at the counter, he picked his phone from its holster. He thought that a few more sympathies thrown his way would be good for his psyche. When he checked the news site, he saw that his comment was gone, as were all of the comments on his comment. A bit of a cold chill ran through him at that moment, but he shook it off. Maybe something had offended the moderator. He had been real frank about his thoughts. Barry went back to the toaster.

The toast hadn't moved the fuel needle much, and the visibility of the pantry bottoms would keep him hungry until a round trip to the store. The grocery was only a couple blocks, but he jumped into the Volvo anyway. The oversleep had cramped his legs. In the grocery, a stranger poked him in the back as he stood in the checkout lane. Barry glanced behind himself to see the front of the man's cart, now pulled back a foot or so. "Sorry," came from the man - an older fellow - maybe in his eighties. "No problem." Barry went back to his reverie, watching the lady in front of him place items on the belt. Seemingly in obsessive compulsive fashion, she gingerly placed each item, label fronted, and spaced equidistantly on the belt. For a couple minutes she did this, and then the elderly gent spoke again.

"We reserve the right to censor attacks against the state."

Barry twisted around, flushing with anger. The man barely changed the fix of his countenance. "Sorry, is there a problem?" Barry relaxed a little, "I don't know."

Back at the apartment, Barry put the sack down on the counter. He was still miffed about the gent at the grocery. The little jab, he realized, was to get his attention, so the Triumvirate lackey could play out his little spiel. Barry whispered to himself, "No doubt the old geezer was being directed by his cell phone nanny mother."

Barry walked back to the bedroom and pulled the luger from his dresser drawer. He brought it to the kitchen, laid out some newsprint, and began to disassemble the gun. It was a habit formed by his short tour on the police force.

Now he looked in dismay at the gun. He picked up the piece, and scrutinized it intensely, holding it a few inches from his eyes. Then he put it back down, as a knock at the door interrupted him. At the door was his keeper - the one with whom he could associate just about everything wrong in his life, but who had become his only real confidant.

In a minute, the two of them sat at the counter. As Cindi munched on a cookie from the bag, Barry spoke first. "How did you get my luger Cindi?"

"We shouldn't talk here Barry."

"It probably doesn't matter anymore Cindi. How did you get the luger?"

Cindi waved her hands, gesturing "Why does it matter?"

"Elliot gave it to me."

Barry let out a long breath. "They're onto us then. It was probably a bad idea for you to come here anyway - today. Why did you?"

Cindi ignored his question. "I'll tell you - but first, why do you think they're onto us?" Barry picked up the piece of his firearm, taking it from the counter, and holding it in front of Cindi. His companion was a police officer - no matter that she was also a pretty brunette - and so her eyes widened when she realized what she was seeing on the gun-part in Barry's hand.

"The firing pin has been filed."

"Yes."

"Great way to set up an unintentional suicide by cop."

"Yes."

"They're evil Barry ... they'll do us like they did Jere. Now she mouthed the words without voicing them, "Barry. We gotta go somewhere else." Then, in a very low voice she added, "A few hours ago, I was getting ready for my shift, and I went into my apartment closet to dress. I heard a strange rattling sound coming from the corner. I thought ... you know ... maybe the plumbing was having a baby again. That's happened. The snake snapped its head up as it uncoiled from between two boxes on the floor. I had a freak'in heart attack - my legs instinctively launched my body out of the closet and into the bedroom, like I was in autopilot long jump mode. My calf muscles still hurt. I called animal control, but then realized that I could no longer live there anyway. I tossed a few of my dearest things into a suitcase, and came here."

Cindi shook her head, "I'm sure they hear every word we say. We haven't been very careful, have we?" Barry snorted, "It's hard to get used to bizzaro world, you know."

Cindi stood up, tossing her head back, and then shouting, "Hey Eliot! Hey Graham! Kiss off you rotten bastards!" Barry walked over to the desk that was built into the corner of the kitchen. He pulled a sheaf of papers from the desk drawer, and then a pen. He walked back to where Cindi sat, examining his gun. Barry sat down with her, and started assembling the weapon.

Cindi wrote onto the paper, "Why bother, if it's ruined?"

Barry smiled at her, taking the pen, and writing "My dad was a machinist. I think I have the genes. All I need is a little grinding wheel."

Barry walked back to the desk, and took a large clasped envelope from the top drawer. He brought it back to Cindi, and handed it to her. Cindi mouthed no words, but pulled the contents from the envelope. It was from Alicia's lawyer. Cindi read a few paragraphs from the top page and reinserted the packet back into the envelope, saying in a whispered voice, "I'm sorry."

Now Barry wrote on the paper, "I'll put together a few things. Give me a little while." Cindi nodded, and Barry went through his dresser drawer, pulling a couple items from his closet, a few more from the desk drawer, and tossing all of them into a medium sized piece of luggage. He had no choice, as it was the only bag that Alicia had not taken. It was the one he normally used, and so she probably wanted nothing to do with it.

Barry took his cell phone, walked over to the kitchen sink, and shoved the gray-black device down into the garbage disposal. He reached over and threw the switch. A noise - harsh, metallic and disturbing, emanated from the disposal. He turned to look at Cindi's surprised face. "I've been wanting to do that for a while."

The two of them walked out of the door, and down to the street where Cindi's car was parked. After Barry deposited the suitcase on the rear seat, he took his place on the passenger side of Cindi's Buick. He pulled a sheaf of papers from his rear pocket, and waved the pen at Cindi. "No doubt" were her only words as she slid the key home, engaged the motor, and pulled out of the cul-de-sac. Shortly, they were flying down the Boulevard and across the midtown bridge.

When they reached the church parking lot next to the storage facility, Barry looked at Cindi. Incredulous, he mouthed the words without saying them, "You're kidding." Cindi similarly mouthed words, "No choice, Bubalouie."

In almost the same instant, the one already and other soon to be ex-cop noticed that they were not alone in the parking lot. A bulky car was positioned half the length of the lot from them, and a first glance seemed to indicate it was empty. As the twosome watched the vehicle in the early dawn light, they noticed the slight movements made by some persons within the vehicle. Those occupants had slowly slouched down on their seats, so that their heads were barely perceptible across the top of the hood.

Barry wrote on the paper, "Amateurs."

Cindi wrote back, "No doubt. Citizen/Triumvirate patrol. Checking us out. Apparently, they know we come here regularly."

Barry responded with the pen, "The locals don't realize we have running on our minds, or they'd have sent better than these ..."

Cindi turned and noiselessly mouthed "They don't think we can!"

Barry pulled the gun from his holster, and opened the door. Cindi forgot to write and instead blurted out, "What are you doing with that!?"

"They won't know it's broken, Cindi." Then, he took the pen from her hand, and wrote down the words, "If they see the scooter, we're screwed." Cindi appreciated his statement, and lamented that "of all the things I should have thrown into my case, you'd have thought that my gun would have been on the list ..."

Cindi followed Barry across the lot to the other car. Cindi flashed her badge, and Barry stood next to the window, motioning for the occupants to roll it down. Barry knew that these blokes would have no guns. They would never give real bullets to these Dudleys. As the window came down, Barry put the luger in the driver's face. "You don't need to die today. If you comply, you'll be OK." Barry noticed the passenger slowly moving his hand over to his cell phone clip. Barry advised him, "You'll put your hands on the dash, or this will be your day."

"We're under the black hat now Barry."

"No choice."

The twosome herded their captives up along the side of the church, and then next to the iron window bars of the church window, on the side opposite from the storage facility. While Barry held the luger on them, Cindi retrieved a couple of handcuffs.

Chuckling now, "I've always kept these in my car. Now I know why."

While Barry steadily trained the gun between the bigger one's eyes, Cindi secured a cuff pair onto each prisoner, attaching one end to the iron bar on the window, and the other end to the captive. Barry noted that the prisoners would eventually be freed, saying, "Should be somebody here to worship God before you two starve to death. While you're biding your time, maybe you should say a prayer or two. You're on the wrong side from-" Barry pointed upwards.

In the storage bay, the twosome traded ideas about what to take and what to leave. Neither could take even the small amount that had been hurriedly tossed into the luggage cases. The saddle bags bulged as they pushed in their selections. After Cindi plugged the jammer into the battery clip, Barry finally spoke out loud, "Gawd, I'd hate to be a mute. It's a bitch."

Then he added. "So, crazy bad motor scooter rider. Where are we going?"

"West. Someplace with a low population density. Someplace we can get our acts together, and not be bitten by venomous snakes or become involved in a rigged game of shootout."

"On this moped?" Barry was incredulous.

"No choice Bubalouie. No choice." Cindi pulled a couple printed maps from her pocket. "I've had half-assed thoughts about this kind of escape for a long time, even before you came along Barry. That's why you saw me packing those compact bicycle rider's items, like the tent." Now she waved the maps in the air. "These are bicycle trail maps, and suggested secondary route maps for bicycle riders. We can do this, so long as we give Betsy lots of breaks for carrying our bums. We need to lay low anyway."

Barry walked up to the bike, and patted the windshield. "Anything you want Betsy."

The first ten miles put the wind on their left. It was a fierce blast of wind, and so they rode along in silence. Barry felt uncomfortable about putting his arms around Cindi. He held them as loosely as he could, while steadying himself. Barry could easily see over her shoulder - he could almost see over the top of her head - and he noticed that the speedo was stuck at forty two, even with the the blast of wind on their left and a little at their backs.

Finally the scooter made its first course change, putting the wind fully at their backs, and making conversation possible.

"I can't believe we're doing this. It's insane."

"Barry, I thought I already informed you, the world is crazy. Remember?"

Barry thought about what he had left at the apartment. "I

didn't have much to leave behind Cindi, except for Alicia. I don't know about you."

"Same."

Cindi corrected herself. "No - not the same. I'm leaving a heaping pile of stinking dirt, and the dirtbags who play in it. You have no idea Bubalouie."

Barry waited a moment, then said "Why do so many go along with it?"

Cindi took a second to formulate her thoughts, then said "There's a difference between freedom and what I have been sloshing around in for the past three years. They give these people SUVs and tell them it makes them free. If they can occasionally buy the high-end latte on the menu, they are told that makes them free. Really Barry, it's Satan's tail of narcissism poking them in their own asses. It's the materialism that has killed their souls, and brainwashed their minds. At the end of the day, we have the wrong end of the horse in our faces. It has been the cause for this country, and the rest of the world - in my opinion - to fall under an authoritarian dictatorship run by educated, suit wearing criminals. Our legislature was done in by its own corruption, blackmailed by people even more vile and corrupt. I feel like extracting myself from society, so that I can just watch it kill itself from afar - while eating my potato chips, and sharing a drink with a real close friend. Maybe someone like you. "

Three hours later the moped crossed the state line. As they entered the first town, Cindi pulled the little cycle into the parking lot of a *Road Warrior* gasoline station. She walked up to the front of the little convenience store attached to the station, and plugged some quarters into the newspaper vending machine. Then she motioned for Barry to follow her to the employee's lunch-break bench. It was perched on the end of the concrete pad, just past the ice cube machine and around the corner of the little storefront. Barry sat down with her. He found himself grinning when he looked at her, and then said "You're fascinating."

"Fascinating? What am I - a bug? Barry, you're a smart guy. I don't want to breath down on you or anything. It's just that I've been plotting this for a while, and I've considered some of the travails that I ... err ... I mean ... we might run into. Let me explain. Our state allows mopeds to be unlicensed. This state requires a license. We don't want to attract any attention, do we?"

"Guess not."

Cindi began jotting down notes and addresses. Soon she had a list of ten addresses. Barry noticed she had the page turned to the classified section.

"Fascinating. Just fascinating."

Barry decided not to ask. He would just follow along. "Why look stupid?" he thought.

The first address was a nondescript cape cod on the end of a street in the older section of town. The little sign in the yard sparked Barry's interest. On the sign was scrawled, along with a phone number, "Moped for sale."

The woman who answered the door had a cane, and Barry guessed she was not the rider. Cindi asked a few questions about the bike. Then she asked, "Why are you selling it?" "My husband passed away a year ago, and I don't ride, as you might imagine."

"Sorry about your husband. I think we may be interested in

the moped. Can we see it?"

"I'm not very mobile, give me a second and I'll get the key for you. It's in the garage."

A couple minutes later, Cindi had unlocked the door at the side of the garage, and she and Barry entered the little space. "Whew - musty in here."

"Probably hasn't seen fresh air in a year or more, Barry. It's perfect!"

"Perfect? You're fascinating. Why is this one better than Betsy?"

"It's not better than Betsy. This one has a small motor. It'll not do for us." Then Cindi pulled a little screwdriver from her purse, and stooped down at the back of the moped. Thirty seconds later, the little moped license plate was in her purse."

"Thief."

"OK. You call the police. See ya later." Cindi started walking back to the front entrance of the little house. She handed the key back, and Barry heard her say something about its being too small. "I'm so sorry it won't work for you," was the reply from the old lady.

Cindi waited until Betsy had backtracked a dozen blocks before she stopped to put the plate on the moped. "The reason it was perfect Barry?"

Barry was happy to exhibit some intelligence. He had been feeling a little underpowered. "Because the old lady won't know or remember anything about a plate, and the buyers will expect to get their own."

"Very good." Now Cindi was smiling. "It helps to know a little bit about police matters, I guess. Moped plates in this state are good for five years."

Now, the twosome resumed their secondary road route, bypassing any further tour of the town. They stopped often to give Betsy a break. It was late afternoon when they entered the state forest. "Probably some rough trails here. It says on the bike guide that there are some creek bed walkovers, and that some of them are impassible, depending upon the time of year."

Cindi looked back at Barry in the rear view, and he nodded.

It was near dusk when they reached the first creek bed. They dismounted the moped, and Cindi tried to stay within a few feet of it. The creek bed had water. "Too hard to tell how deep it is in the dark - we should wait till morning."

Barry agreed. They set up a camp, and put the moped on the end of the tent, so that the jammer could do its job.

Cindi said "They'll know we were at the old lady's place, of course. That's not necessarily a big deal, since we're almost a hundred miles away now. But, we can't let it happen very often, because they'll plot our trajectory."

"How do we get you unchained from this thing?"

"A doctor."

"You know one who'll do it?"

"I have the ... you know ... drunken philanderer talk to go by. Over the years I kept hearing one name consistently. One guy said he'd had it done, probably so that he could be a philanderer."

"Where?"

"St Louie."

"We're going in the wrong direction then."

"Not that Saint Louie. One more state line to go."

"Licensed mopeds?"

"Unilateral reciprocal agreement."

"Nice. How'd you get to be so g-damned smart?"

Now Cindi smiled at him. "What are you buttering me up for, Bubalouie?"

"I'm not sure I like being a Bubalouie. Doesn't seem like a very bright guy." Cindi's smile got bigger. One side of her face scrunched up just a little. Then, in a much softer voice, she said "OK, Barry."

The little spot next to the creek bed was a biker's favorite. This fact was evidenced by the rock ring. The charred wood pieces that littered its perimeter were evidence too - indicating a recent traveler's fire and overnight stay.

Cindi started a little fire, and Barry took a spot next to the ring. The air was not cold, but the fire seemed comforting in some way ... Barry imagined in the very same way that it would have been comforting to an Indian sitting near the same spot five hundred years earlier. There was something about the power of it, lashing out with its little flashes and sparks, keeping the evil spirits away.

Cindi went to the saddle bag, and retrieved something in a

small bag. "I've made some dinner for us."

"You're amazing."

Cindi stooped over the fire, and handed the strip to Barry.

"Yum. Beef Jerky. You're quite a talent."

"Keep it up Bubalouie."

"Now I'm Bubalouie."

"Eat your dinner."

Barry started munching on his jerky, making all manner of noise to indicate his enjoyment of his meal.

Cindi's face was dour, "I think tomorrow Betsy's gonna have a lighter load to carry."

"You'd leave me to the bears, would you?"

Cindi relaxed and let out a quick breath. Nah - you might prove to be useful. She stood up, walked to the tent, took off her clothes, and hung them over the tent wires. She crouched down, crawled into the tent, and laid down on the biker's sleeping bag.

Five minutes later, Barry slowly stood up from his spot next to the ring. Cindi could hear him walking away from the camp. She could hear some rustling sounds, but not of animals. Of him. Then, she could hear the splash.

When Cindi emerged from the tent in the morning, she noticed Barry sleeping on the ground next to the ring. She kicked his boot. "Seems you have a few hangups Bubalouie. I always sleep nude."

"I'm not sure how this is working."

"At least you're clean. Speaking of which-" Cindi walked

naked down to the creek bed. From his spot next to the ring, he watched the back of her form as she washed ...

6

Saint Louie

Betsy was seriously in need of a break. After Cindi knocked down the kickstand, she put her hand on the side of the motor, and extracted it with a violent motion. "Hot! Sixty miles without a break. We shouldn't do that again." Saint Louie was not a small town, and not a big one either. "Population 17,000" was boldly proclaimed on the corporation limit sign they passed on the ride into the village.

Cindi lingered near the jammer, while Barry went into the store. He sauntered up to the counter saying, "I'd like some direction."

"I can point you to any local bar. Beyond that, no guarantees," the man said as he laughed. "We're looking for a doctor. Goes by the name Walt or Walter - we're not sure." The storekeep glanced out the front window at Cindi. "Wish my girlfriend looked like that."

"She won't be your girlfriend for long if she hears that."

Cindi watched the banter, as it went back and forth, through the window. She noticed that they were spending a lot of time looking at her. It seemed they were having a good time. Finally, Barry walked out to the bike. Cindi slitted her eyes.

"It better have been good Bubalouie."

"We only said nice things about you."

Dr. Walter's office was in his home, about a mile outside of the city limit, on the west end of town. He was obviously a very old man. The appreciation of this fact registered on the young couple's faces, and it was cause for a chuckle from the doctor. "Yes, I'm a pretty old guy."

Cindi told the doctor that she had an implant she wanted removed. She didn't know what to expect from the man, as she explained her situation, and was relieved to see that his expression barely changed. He was nonplussed. "Yes, that's about all I do anymore. I really don't practice. How did you know about me?" Barry was relieved that Cindi came up with an alternate story for the doctor. "You're wise to come to me, young lady. The bastards put barbs on those things - you'd cut yourself apart trying to do it in your bathroom."

The procedure didn't take long. The doctor's years may have put him on the edge of ancient, but the talent was still in his fingers. Twenty minutes later, Cindi held her tormentor in her hand. The bloodied little thing was but the size of a pea, less the barbs that spread out behind it. The doctor said, "You two seem like a good couple. I'd like to invite you to a little get-together this evening, with some other people in your boat, so to speak. You'll find comfort in the shared stories, I'm sure."

Barry and Cindi thanked the doctor, and promised to return to his house at the designated time.

Just before seven, Barry's knock was answered by an older woman. She seemed younger than the doctor, and they were unsure how to address her. The woman solved their dilemma, saying "I'm Walter's wife. Please come in."

The group contained about twenty people ... but that was more than Barry had expected. They sat around on sofas and chairs and just about anything else they could find. All were already munching on various foods that had been prepared, and soon Barry and Cindi were having their fill of the same. "No offense," Barry said to Cindi, "but this may just barely edge out the jerky." "Ha! Liar!" shot back from a feisty Cindi. Barry was constantly amazed that even with all that had happened, Cindi could still wear the shutzpah. Suddenly she touched his shoulder, "Barry."

"Hey, you know my name again!"

"No. Really, look at all of those people eating."

"Yeah. It has to be done occasionally. I've found this to be true myself."

"Dummy. No, look at *how* they're eating."

"They're hungry. By the way, I prefer Bubalouie."

"Crap. You notice nothing, BUBALOUIE!" They're all left handed. Every single one!

Barry took notice. "That's pretty weird."

Cindi cocked her head to one side. "You're an analyst."

Later, after the young couple - easily the youngest of any of

the attendees, had made the rounds, greeting each of the other guests, they found themselves again standing next to the doctor's wife. Cindi spoke to her, "You know, it's an odd thing, in a way, but it seems that all of your guests are left handed. Mrs. Walter looked at them and smiled. "Yes."

Barry and Cindi exchanged glances. The doctor's wife looked at Barry. "Barry, are you left handed?" Barry's head nodded up and down.

The lady turned to Cindi, saying "you?"

Now Cindi's head was moving up and down.

"Pretty suspicious, isn't it? I'm sorry, I'm not making fun of you. I guess we all need a little levity in these times, do we not?"

"The doctor will explain it to you."

A while later, the crowd had thinned to a dozen or so. Barry and Cindi had been spending their time taking in the conversations, but participating only a little. Occasionally, they had reason to nod, as the words they heard spoken conveyed patches of meaning for puzzle pieces they had already played, out of their own experience.

Finally, the group had narrowed to eight, and the doctor took over the conversation. Looking directly at Barry and Cindi, he said "We have been allowing you to pick up on things so much as is your inclination. You may think we're all crazy."

"No. We're both hearing many familiar things."

"Well - good." He chuckled. "No - not really good. What a thing to say. But, now we know where to start with you. You're familiar with the Triumvirate?"

"Yes - through the impeccable descriptions of a drunken defense contractor."

There was unified laughter. From the corner came, "I like these two. A sense of humor is why we're all still alive."

Once more the chuckles reverberated though the group.

The doctor stood up, and held out his hand to the young couple. "Why don't you tell us about the course that brought you here. That seems likely to take less time than the other way around. About a half hour later, Barry finished with "That's about it - plus or minus."

The doctor's face lost most of its humor. "Our world is in a great deal of trouble. You seem to have had many experiences that should point you to that conclusion, but we could add many more in the next minutes and hours that might very well be cause for you to conclude that ..." The doctor let himself slip back into his chair. "... that might make you think to give up."

"Not really the giving up kind."

"Good."

The doctor leaned forward in his chair. "It started with our own technology and our own government people. Publicly, we had of course, the most brilliant technology in the world, in the view of most people. That technology was eclipsed by a hidden, far more powerful government version."

"From the beginning, they made heavy use of technology to fight crime, to protect agents, and to shine light in places that conventional technology could not. This was well and good. One of the first ideas that came out of this environment was the *fuzz ball*. The fuzz ball was a small chip hidden in a piece of lint, and put into agent's ears. This gave agents very well cloaked full communications capabilities even before the cell phone was available to the public. Lives were saved because the criminals did not discover that agents were wired without wires.

Then, the brilliant idea came along to hide the devices completely by burying them in the flesh. Cindi here knows all about that. It eventually got down to the level of street cops -

at least those in certain positions. They weren't very discriminate, and the criminals eventually caught on. I can tell you very gruesome stories about some agents for which the devices were not protective."

"One thing that *outed* the devices was the fact that our agents sometimes had to go to the hospital, and when they did, the government doctors did not always have control of the situation.

More and more of the medical establishment became aware of the practice. Eventually, that would include myself. This had the effect of making agents, if you will, of doctors. Inevitably, there came a time when the majority operated in unison with various agencies as *secret* agents, keeping the truth from the public, and ostensibly for the public good. It forced medical personnel to develop two faces, and yes - to basically lie to the public in many cases. With us so far?" The doctor looked keenly at the couple.

"Yes."

"OK then. This is the problem with secretive agencies that do clandestine operations. Eventually, without proper oversight, they unlearn the distinctions that must be kept between truth and lie."

"About this time, the world was not staying put. Technology was racing ahead at a furious pace. The Soviets and the Chinese engaged in this furious endeavor - to create all the fancy gizmos to do what had not yet been done - usually without any worry about consequences."

"The Soviets were keen upon the reexamination of all the electromagnetic theories. Cindi, your friend told us about the drunken sailor and his tales of the *God Machine*, yes?"

Cindi nodded, and the doctor continued, "The *God Machine* does exist, and if it were trained on us, all hope would indeed be lost. The lucky thing for humanity, and the thing that gives us some time but not an extensive amount of it, is the fact that the God machine is backed by computers that cannot cover every place and every moment. They must prioritize. They look for hot spots. That is why we must be very careful to never, ever, give them reason to add us to their list of priorities. I knew that you understood this, Cindi, when I saw Barry lugging the heavy battery up the walk in front of my house. I felt I could take a chance on you."

"Now, the unfortunate thing for us, in this country, is that while the Soviets were busy gathering fodder for the blackmail of our legislature, our own people were enhancing the implants, and putting them in an ever wider circle of people. Paramedics, for crying out loud. Henry, raise your hand." Henry was the one in the corner who had exhibited some humor via his laughter. Now he smiled. "Paramedic no more, I'm afraid. Would compromise the crew."

The doctor stood up again. "About the same time, a discovery was made, by a European, of an effect caused by the use of cell phones very close to the head. One Dr. Franklin Guard made this discovery, as part of a clandestine military research program for his native European nation. It was discovered, that the amazing human brain could decode information from the electromagnetic wave generated by the phone. Directly! This discovery soon led to the use of the phone's *echo*, as they called it, to subliminally manipulate certain phone users. Those users were, ostensibly, criminals against whom undisclosed charges were pending. I have my doubts. It's the way it always works, it seems." The doctor shook his head.

"The effect is that the signal is processed mostly by the

subconscious brain. It works into the consciousness only in a foggy, imprecise manner. This made it very useful for law enforcement, because it could be used to manipulate criminals into predictable behavior and various bushwhack setups in order to apprehend them.

Evolution taught the conscious mind to be very suspicious of the subconscious, and vice versa. The designers of the *echo* manipulation found that, over time, the *echo* caused a confusion in the differentiation of thoughts originated by the conscious versus the subconscious mind. It caused the normal evolutionary rules to blur. It allowed, in some cases, the unconscious mind - normally filtered and moderated by the conscious mind, to exert some control, and bypass the rational restrictions normally enforced by the thinking, conscious mind.

This is how the Triumvirate was able to lead humanity down the primrose path, so to speak. The real design of the Triumvirate should be seen in its obvious deceit, but the moral compass of the population - the one developed over eons of generations and the evolution of the human brain - was mutated by the *echo* technology. The populace became so misaligned by the effect, that it no longer recognized the deceit of the Triumvirate – the deceit simply failed to register."

Now the doctor was interrupted. Johnny's sandwich was on the floor. His wife was embarrassed for him, and picked it up. The doctor was quick to salve the couples embarrassment. "It's OK Johnny. We have plenty more." The doctor's wife hurried off to the kitchen to retrieve a replacement.

"Johnny here *is a doctor*, and you can see he has a severe case of Parkinsons. He got too many doses of the neuro-toxin that they use. You see, Johnny was very outspoken about his reservations about the new *system*. They made a target of him."

Cindi and Barry exchanged glances. The doctor raised his eyebrows. "Well, Barry started, "I've been on the wrong end of one of their guns."

"How many times?"

"Once."

"You're OK. It takes about fifty doses."

Barry nodded, "So, they're slowly murdering people?"

"Yes. I took the Hippocratic oath a long time ago, but Johnny here knows his situation very well. Johnny was, and is, a very good doctor. He has about two years, in both our estimations." Johnny's head jerked enough to qualify as an acknowledgment of what Walter said, but in a very pained and awkward way.

The doctor continued, "They key on some natural hatreds to more effectively manipulate the people. Think about a natural instinct or reflex - often it is the domain of the subconscious mind, so the channel is more open for it, and they use it. Some people have been so manipulated by this phenomenon that they no longer think for themselves.

We refer to them as the *echo slaves*."

"We're not going to overload you with information. Tomorrow you will meet a very special person. That is ... if you accept our invitation to stay with us. We hope that you will."

The doctor's wife interjected, "We have three rooms ... your choice."

7

Franciscan

Louise, the doctor's wife, walked up the steps ahead of the couple. As she reached the top landing of the double stairs, she waved down the hall, "Any of the three on the left are yours. Just let me know if you need anything." She smiled and retreated down the stairs.

As they passed the first open door, Barry turned to Cindi. "That's yours. It's pink." Barry walked to the second opening, and turned back to Cindi. Chuckling under his breath, "It's lavender, but I guess it'll be fine. I like the price."

Barry had just settled down under the comforter on the bed. The room was luxurious, appointed with the best that could be bought. The mattress under him was firm and solid, unlike the cheap one he had slept on for years, and shared with Alicia. Even with the weight of the crazy world and crazy stories told by crazy doctors living in an insane world run by homicidal lunatics, Barry was soon on the cusp of a much needed slumber. Unfortunately for Barry, a rude bounce from the mattress knocked him out of the slow, fuzzy-soft prelude to his sleep. Opening his eyes, he could see that Cindi had dropped her not unpleasant derrière onto the bed next to him. "How can you sleep after what just happened?"

"Believe me, I can sleep. I was just about to do that, BUBALOUIE!"

"You know, I think the doctor's wife thought we would need only one room. She had a sort of twinkle in her eye."

"No. Those were tears. She knew you were going to ruin my nice sweet sleepy dreams by sitting on my bed, and talking about stuff I'd really just like to forget."

"If you'd bother to look, it could be that sometimes I have a twinkle in my eye."

"I'll bet you always ask the boys for dates, dontcha?" Although it was not his intent or desire, the conversation soon turned into a long boring history of Barry's love life, his wife, and the reason that he felt compelled to walk to the second door. Now Cindi looked at him. The low light seeped in from the hallway and reflected her facial expression into his eyes. It made transparent all of the disbelief in the mind behind her pretty complexion.

"You haven't made love to your wife in almost three years!? That's real crazy, Bubalouie Barry."

"It's really none of your business either. My love life hasn't been up to snuff maybe, but it isn't Alicia's fault. The person whose fault it is probably shares a bunk with some other dude, and I dream that they look out of the bars together every morning. One smiling. One not."

Barry tilted his head, "You know, it's all relative. Many people die before their sixteenth birthday and their first wet kiss. Guess I'm lucky ... relatively speaking. It's not all about sex darling."

Cindi looked at the form lying on the bed. She had known many men. This guy was different ... just so different. Now her voice note changed to the off-key sharp - the tenor of resignation. "That's what I always do, compare myself to the least privileged. Sure, that'll always make me feel better. Yeah - and what about all the starving Chinese children?"

"Let them starve and me sleep. Please."

Cindi walked to the door, slowly, making very sure that Barry could see what he was missing.

"I didn't look, darling."

The morning brought eggs, bacon, and the realization in the two guests that Louise had as much culinary skill in her fingers as her husband had surgical skill in his. Finally, when they had finished, the doctor stood up from the table. "Do you remember anything from last night, or was it a bad dream?" Barry looked at the doctor, then his wife, saying "I can't decide." The doctor's wife came round the table and touched Barry's shoulder. "Dreams can't touch."

Across the table, the doctor nodded his head up and down, saying, "Unfortunately."

The catholic priest arrived about eleven o'clock, and was ushered into the den, the place of the previous night's activities. "Father Preston couldn't be here last night. He'd like to have a little talk with the two of you, if that's OK?"

Cindi smiled, extending a hand to the padre, and the foursome positioned themselves in such a way as to give the priest a spot at the head of the table.

The doctor introduced his comments, saying, "Father Preston will be speaking about things you may find difficult to believe. Please just take in what he has to say, and digest it for a while, before you decide whether or not he and I are both ... crazy."

The padre stood up, back stepped a few feet, leaning against the wall behind himself. He looked pointedly at Barry, then Cindi, and asked "What is the soul?"

Barry looked surprised, but regained his thoughts and formulated a response. "It's ... a spiritual, invisible, essence that represents our eternal selves ... it's what we really are, outside of our bodies."

"You could have read that from a catechism of your grade school days, young man!"

"I did."

"You're Catholic?"

Barry's face turned color, and he looked embarrassed. The elderly priest put out a short "I see."

"You've joined the ranks of the present day world, my son. It's not entirely your fault. The peer pressure is a massive distraction. That's intentional."

"For thousands of years, Satan has been looking for a hook into the psyche of humanity ... a direct connection to them ... a communications pathway directly into their minds. Up until recently, he has been able to interest people only in a very abstract, diffused sort of way. He has been able only to marginally manipulate the movers and shakers - in places such as Hollywood - and inside of the centers of cultural power - in order to shift popular thinking towards the end paradigm that suits him. He wanted more control, and we believe that recent discoveries have finally given it to him.

Barry looked at the old priest. He tried to wipe the patronizing look of fake belief from his face, but he could feel the muscles inside of his cheeks, and knew that they had not managed to convincingly comply with his wishes.

"It's OK Barry. Just remember to digest all of this later. Take your time."

"In grade school, we talk about the soul. It's a diffused definition that we give it, isn't it Barry? You know what? In high level post seminary education - the priest gets no better an explanation! We get the same explanation as what you - so excellently - remembered from your catechism. In theology classes, we sat around and talked about it. What is the soul, we asked ourselves. Officially, we must quote the dogma and embrace it, even with its inherent fuzziness. It's the way it is. This is what we say. But, like I said, we sat around in groups and postulated beyond the official doctrine. Especially when we are young, we naturally think a little outside of the boundaries, right? It was many years ago for me, but I remember. We decided that it was some kind of energy - a coherent, collected sort of energy with the ability to be cognizant about things."

"Sounds crazy, doesn't it?"

"Science these days leans against the concept of matter entirely. The new thought is that only energy exists! If only energy exists, then how crazy is it to say that the soul is energy?"

The priests took a rubber ball from his pocket, then a fishing weight from the other.

"The long and short of it - is that we do not know what the soul is. Just as is the case with hard science - where - in spite of many PhDs, we do not know what energy is. We do not know what electricity is, and we do not know what matter is! We only know what it does, how it feels, and how it looks. That's all. We know, for certain, nothing else."

"We have created elaborate theories, backed by even more elaborate logical and mathematical constructs, in order to predict the bahaviour of such things as matter and energy, inside of the universe ... and these theories have often worked well to be our tools and to do our bidding, heating our houses, allowing us to communicate with our peers, and to send people to the moon. These theories always have one thing in common. They are always conjectures pointed at the prediction of effect, and when the effect happens as predicted, we say that the theories are true. Yet, as twenty or fifty or a hundred years pass, we find that the educated definitions we had applied ... the theories ... prove false. The official doctrine routinely turns out to be false, and when that happens we substitute other theories that describe another piece of conjecture ... maybe particles of particles of particles of particles, when - in fact - we don't know if there are any particles at all. Maybe it's just energy.

"Maybe the soul is energy."

"If the soul is energy, then what might be the best way to communicate with it? Maybe, with some other form of energy?"

"Some of us think so. We call it the Devil's Conduit, and the people who created it *Beelzebub's Bargain*. They purchased for Satan the one thing he could not produce himself - a connection to the human soul."

Barry's blank face said it all. "You're all crazy," it beamed into the room.

The priest's facial expression was that of a teacher. "You'll come along, it seemed to be saying. Now he spoke, "You think we're crazy. I know. Most days, until about noon or so, I think I'm crazy. Then the reality hits again. We are living in the last days, my friend."

"Doctor Walt has some information that may help you to digest what we are talking about."

The doctor stood up. "Let's go to the dining room. It'll be easier." The foursome moved to the kitchen, and the doctor pushed a file cart along behind the others. Finally, they were all situated around the table.

Doctor Walt advised, "I've another friend who will be arriving shortly. He should be able to add some technical substance to what Father Preston and I will be saying."

The doctor started laying out newspapers, with headlines circled. The first was about a cell phone executive who had thrown himself out of his sixteenth floor executive office, in front of horrified witnesses both in his office and on the street below. Another headline concerned a fellow by the name of Geo Dennison, and Barry interjected a comment about how he had watched the eleven o'clock news report on the night it happened. The doctor kept pulling papers, and soon there were a dozen different articles spread out upon the table.

"These were not regular suicides, Barry, Cindi." Some of these were far too gruesome to be the act of a normal person. People who kill themselves simply don't do these things. One cell exec had cut his own legs off with a chain saw, and bled to death. Other examples were as bad.

From Barry, "Why isn't the press pulling this together?"

"Isn't that an interesting question, Barry?" "We do have the reports of the deaths, here in these clippings. But, nowhere is there printed any type of alarm, calling for any kind of investigation, in spite of the fact that these suicides have caused a nearly complete replacement of all the top people in the communications industry. It's insane! I'll admit, the deaths are over a sixteen year period, and the public memory is short."

"Six months." Barry felt good to add something to the conversation. "We were told that in my forensics classes. After six months, the public completely forgets."

The elderly gents both nodded.

"So, what does this mean?"

"Let me show you a video." The doctor pulled another cart from the corner of the room. On it was a small LCD monitor screen, and on its first shelf was a laptop computer. The doctor fiddled with the computer, and now it displayed a video. The video showed a man walking down the street. This man passed another man, who seemed to be waiting on a corner. It was clear that the bouncing video was taken by someone on foot, following at some distance. As the first man, wearing a red shirt, passed the one who was waiting, the second man spun around. The face of the second man twisted into convulsion, its muscles spasming and contorting the cheeks. The second man, it seemed to Barry, had become possessed ... taken over by something ... temporarily replaced in the manner of an old Hollywood movie. The thing that the second man had become screamed, "You filthy animal!" It twisted its head, snarling at the red shirted man. Its countenance changed continuously, the muscles hardening and convulsing out of shape. Now it seemed to Barry that its head had taken the shape of a jackal's head. It swung its fist wildly, landing one on the poor man's face. The man fell backwards onto the concrete walk. The red shirted man pushed himself up on one elbow, then fell back. Blood gushed from the victim's mouth, and as his jaw fell hard against the pavement, he cried out in pain. In an instant, the second man's face resumed a natural look. He turned his back to the injured man, and walked away. He walked slowly ... normally ... never turning back.

The doctor stood and went back to the cart. He clicked the mouse, and the video went blank.

"Barry. Was it human?"

Barry said nothing.

"We believe that what you just witnessed was a bona fide case of possession Barry. We believe that the people who created this system no longer control it. We believe control has been wrested from them. We believe many and most likely the majority of the people who originally created and controlled this system are dead. What you just witnessed is happening more and more frequently. Our videotape was fortuitous, but it's not a lone example."

"Maybe there was another reason why the second one was so angry at the first?"

"Yes. That's likely."

"What then?"

"We don't know."

Barry's blank look resumed. The doctor continued, "The original controllers had been using the *echo* system as a method for *social cleansing*, of what they referred to as *undesirables*. They used the subliminal messaging system to create, in the echo slaves, fixations against certain groups of people. Hatreds. They did this because they knew the instinctive emotions of hate could bypass the moral restrictions and inhibitions that the echo slaves would otherwise have. It's how they convinced many of them to do what was done to Johnny."

"Their system is no longer controlled by them. That which controls the system now has a completely different agenda. Different, but decidedly not better. Much worse."

"We think that what controls the echo slaves now also controls the Triumvirate."

There was a knock at the door, and Louise answered it. Shortly, the bald headed Lindsay Kidde entered the dining room. The doctor introduced him, saying "This is Lindsay Kidde. He came to us ten years ago, a refugee of sorts." Lindsay smiled at the doctor and the friar, then turned to Barry and Cindi, saying "I take it these are the newest members of our little circle?" He held out his hand, shaking both of theirs in succession. The doctor sat down, and opened his palm out towards Lindsay, queuing him to start.

"I was a tech setup guy for a big outfit. One day they brought me in to do a little special projects work - R&D type stuff. They told me to set up two cell phones. You may not know, but the cell phone is not a rigid device. Unlike the old types of circuits that were always hard wired to a specific purpose, the cell phone is built so that it can be modified in almost every aspect of its operation - simply by programming the thing. It's pretty amazing. In any case, they asked me to make one phone work so that it would operate normally, excepting for one thing. If it received a specially tagged text message, then it was to simply rebroadcast a voice synthesized analog signal of the message from itself. If it received a specially tagged voice signal, it would simply rebroadcast it as an old-style analog signal. I was puzzled by what they were doing. It seemed to make no sense at all, really, in terms of the woman being able to use the phone."

Lindsay repeated the detail of the experiment, conducted ten years prior, and he described the woman's response, which was tapping the top of her head on a command she could not possibly have heard from the man behind the glass. Lindsay continued, "It was a strange thing to witness - almost like a supernatural effect. The woman responded to the project leader's command even when nothing came from her own headset but her mother's voice! I'm the sorta guy - when something puzzles me like this, I don't let go. I mean, it will bug me until I figure out something that at least makes sense to me, if not anybody else."

"Well, I started looking into it. I started poking around. I worked for a contractor who put me out to various jobs, but I regularly came back to the MagintorCorp Cellular place. Unfortunately, they noticed my nosiness. You understand, at the time I had no reason to expect such blackness as our group now embraces as truth. So, I wasn't very careful. I *borrowed* a very expensive piece of equipment from my company, to run some little experiments of my own, on my own time. I didn't know it at the time, but my little experiments were monitored. They didn't really let on that they knew about what I was doing, but instead made some advance to me about how important I was ... that security was an issue, and so forth. They talked me into the implant. The G-damned thing was barbed! No matter about that. Thanks to the doctor, it's gone. Anyway, I managed to convince myself, by the measurements I was taking, something about that little setup in the little room with the lady and the table and the one-way glass. That experiment was being duplicated on the street every day. I was astounded to find that I could detect old style analog signals, which had no communications purpose anymore – at least as far as I could tell – almost everywhere! They had insinuated my little setup into the public cell system!

I kept digging, and finally I realized that the whole damned thing is some type of system for subliminal control. I spent a lot of time thinking about it. I knew the field strength of a cell phone, operating while held in close contact with the skull, was over 45 v/m. I reasoned that such a strong signal - at Gigahertz frequencies, might interfere in some way, with the brain itself. It seemed intuitive and at the same time crazy as hell."

The doctor interjected, "I've spoken to them already about the echo effect." Lindsay nodded, "OK." There's not much more to my story, other than a half dozen attempts on my life. Twice, I was nearly run over by fast driven automobiles on lonely stretches of street. It was patently obvious to me that the intent was hit and run. Fortunately my legs had enough spring left in them to let me avoid the bastards. Ten years ago they did, but probably not now. I imagined the crazies were executing echoed orders, and afterwards wouldn't have remembered running me down. Eventually I realized that the implant would get me killed, because it made the attempts to harm me frivolously easy, thanks to their knowledge of where I could be found at any hour – and especially – when I was most vulnerable. So, I sought out the good doctor here, and the rest is history."

Barry spoke his first words in a full half hour, clearing his sticking throat as he did. "You seem like a really smart guy, but Cindi and I ... we just don't know what to think at this point. No offense, but these things are-" Cindi added the words, "Strange - very strange."

Lindsay smiled. "Smart? Ha ha – well, you know, there are days when I feel that I could write the equations that would make time travel worm holes work smoothly ... and other days, finding my name is a problem. It's the neuro-toxins. By the time I realized I had to go on the lam, they had gotten me dozens of times. I'm not to Johnny's stage, thank God. Probably will be some day."

The Friar added, "I'll be praying for you Lindsay." He turned to the skeptical youths, "You know, most people don't really want to believe that we're each just a galactic happenstance of random matter and/or energy that seems to have enough intellect to ask itself, "Do I have intellect?" Nor do they want to believe that we'll just fade away some day, that the sun will supernova, and it will be as if we never existed. The will of the people to think beyond that scenario is the reason I put these special clothes on every day, the reason I prepare my sermons, and the reason I bother with anything at all!" The Friar started pacing back and forth, slowly, as if waiting for a response from one of the two young people.

"In recent years, there has been a falling away. The last couple generations have become mostly agnostic and apathetic towards religion. Yet, deep down inside, the fallen away ones haven't lost the intrinsic yearning inside of them - the indefatigable feelings associated with going on beyond our earthly existence some day, and the need to believe in something other than a dead end."

"What they have substituted for their religion, and for their God is-"

"-is the echo! See that the gates of hell have been reopened, and the master manipulator allowed to mainline his message into the   subconsciousness of the fallen away ones, every waking and every sleeping moment."

"Yes, I'm talking about Old Soul - the originator of treachery!"

"Think about it. I could sit here and say to you, I'm the oldest soul in this universe. I'm the one described to you in Genesis, the one cast down with five thousand other fallen ones, eons ago. Worship me, and I will make you powerful ... or sexy ... or rich."

"You'd tell me to go back from whence I came. You probably wouldn't believe me."

"But now you embrace a technology. It has become a part of you that you can't live without. You're addicted to it - messaging your friends, using it constantly. It starts manipulating you, but you are not exactly cognizant of this manipulation, because the messages come through as fuzzy suggestions, like a simulation of your guardian angel, sitting behind your right shoulder. You are oblivious to the fact that it's Beelzebub sitting on your left. This is the way it's working with the echo slaves!"

Barry and Cindi sat there, with sunken cheek bones. The Friar knew the look. He had seen it on the thousands of the near lost - the ones who still bothered to come to church, but who did not receive the word ... the thousands of the distracted ones, ripe for the new and growing army of Beelzebub. He saw them every Sunday. Every Friday and Saturday he scratched and tore away at his own scarce hair, stretching and reaching as he prepared his sermons, searching for the right words he might say, to stop the falling away.

The Friar walked to the corner and picked up his hat and cane from the tree. He turned back to the couple and said "It was nice to meet the both of you. I hope that you can appreciate some of what I've come to say to you."

Cindi was quick to accept the doctor's offer of his truck. She had just been through two of the most bizarre days of her life. She was quickly getting to the point where she didn't believe anything, and she could see the same in Barry. Twenty minutes later, the twosome sat in a booth at a randomly selected burger joint, munching on french fries. Cindi shook her head up and down. "This is more to my liking. There's something real and concrete and believable about a pile of greasy french fries. And ketchup."

Barry laughed. "You know, we can get by for awhile, but eventually we'll need to find a way to buy french fries." Cindi looked around, then surreptitiously scanned the inside of her purse. "I've got about two grand left. Won't starve for a little while."

"The doctor said we could stay for as long as we want."

"Yeah, but then we'd have to listen to his friend's sermons. Man, that was some crazy stuff he was putting out."

"You ever go to church Cindi?"

"Oh yeah - I get it - I'm the immoral fallen away one. You probably can't be seen sitting next to someone of such ill repute!"

"No, really."

"I went when I was a kid. My dad was big on it."

Why didn't we turn out like them?" Cindi shrugged.

"I think we should thank the doctor, and be on our way. I'm thinking Milwaukee."

"Like in freezing ass Wisconsin? No way Bubalouie!"

"We split up then."

"Dummy. She ain't gonna get back with you."

"You're wrong."

Cindi shrugged. "Oh, what the hell. I'm not doing anything else. When do we leave?"

"Tonight."

"OK"

Barry knew something was wrong before he made the last curve on the doctor's private lane. There was a man shuffling back and forth on the road, mumbling something under his breath. He went from one side to the other, and back again, hunched over. He clasped and unclasped his hands, then shook them up and down. His head jerked up as he noticed the doctor's pickup truck and the two young people in it. Now he shouted, "He was warned! Dammit he was warned!"

Cindi advised, "Don't get out of the truck Barry."

"Hey, no problem. This guy's off the end - no doubt."

The man came to the window. He clenched his fists, and shook them menacingly on the other side of the glass. "He was warned!"

Now Barry could see the man's sleeves were stained. There was a large red spot on the front of his trousers, and a streak across the side of his face. Suddenly the fist was slamming against the window. One ... two ... three hard slams, but the window plate glass held. Now the man stopped. He stood there, staring at Barry, his cheeks twitching involuntarily, then stopping, then starting again. Without any indication, he suddenly ran off in the direction of the main road. A couple minutes later, he was out of sight.

Cindi and Barry sat in silence. "My G-"

"Barry. Drive slowly. Be ready to turn this thing around!'

Barry pressed on the pedal lightly. The truck rolled forward, but not so fast as to move the needle off of the peg on the speedo. The doctor had a long, winding drive, and the last curve was a couple hundred feet, ending in a little turn-circle in front of the residence.

Barry stopped the truck in the circle. With big eyes, Cindi twisted around, craning her neck to look over the back of the truck.

"See nothing. How bout you Barry?"

"Nothing."

Barry pulled the door latch inward slowly, as if he were afraid to make any noise as he opened the door ...

Barry stepped out of the truck, walked up to the head of the walk, and waited for Cindi to catch up with him. "No dog."

"Cindi, where's the dog?" The dog had been the relentlessly efficient official announcer of guest arrivals – but now there was no sound. As Barry reached the door, he found it ajar, but closed enough to obscure the interior. Now he felt Cindi brushing his shoulder close up next to him. He turned to look at her, frowning. Cindi raised her eyebrows, then looked down to the threshold of the door.

"Barry." Barry looked back at her. "Look down at your feet

Barry." As Barry complied, he noticed the smear on the polished wooden threshold. "What is it?"

"Dunno. It's wet." Barry reached down, dabbing his finger into the thick end of it, and rubbing his fingers together.

Barry pushed the door ahead. The doctor's entryway and foyer was a straight shot through the dining area to the large multi paned window that normally parceled bright squares of morning sun onto the elderly couple's breakfast table. Now most of the panes were missing, letting the warm outdoor wind blow through them, and through the narrow space of the hallway. The air morphed into a swirl of rotten gas, creating a thick atmosphere fouled by fluids puddled on the floor for the entire length of the building, right up to Barry's feet. Another step and Barry's feet slipped on the wet floor, flipping him backwards into Cindi's chest, sweeping her off of her feet. Cindi went down flat onto her back, sprawling out onto the foyer floor. She reached out to push herself up, but her hands slipped on the slick surface. Barry regained his standing position, and pulled Cindi upright. The latter stared at her hands, her mouth hanging agape. The strength fled her legs as her eyes closed, and she fell limply against Barry, throwing her arms around him. She gripped the sleeve of his right arm, drawing long red streaks along the length of it as she did so.

Barry hustled Cindi over to the base of the stairwell, and helped her up to the first landing, where they came upon the doctor. Walter's lifeless eyes stared up at the ceiling. He was mostly naked, excepting for a profusion of blood and small bits of flesh. Now the forensic specialist in Barry took over, and he observed the several small wounds on the body. It was not the small wounds that were fatal, of course. It was the pike, one that Barry guessed had been pried from the poor doctor's fence, and that was now driven hard into the wooden tread of the stair, and through Walter's body. Cindi fell back down onto the partially carpeted treads, wretching onto them violently.

Barry pulled her to her feet, and then he quickly pushed her up the last three steps and into the hall. Hurriedly, he half pushed, half walked her into the Lavender room, letting her fall onto on the bed there. He dug under the mattress for the luger, and found it. "Stay here!" he commanded, running out of the room, locking the door behind himself. He searched from room to room, looking for others. He covered the entire first floor in less than a minute, then checked the garage and the yard. Another minute, and he was at the Lavender room, without a key. His foot smashed against the jam, sending splinters of broken wood flying into the room along with the strike plate and the screws. He pulled Cindi up by her arms, "We gotta go Cindi - they may be back, and even if they aren't we'll get blamed for this."

Barry strapped Cindi into the pickup truck, locked its doors, and then ran back to the garage where the moped had been parked. He pulled Cindi's cycle back to a place behind the truck, grabbing the front wheel and pulling it up onto the bed. He then moved to the rear of the bike and shoved hard against it to drive it over the top of the bed liner. He ran back to the garage, grabbed the lawn equipment gasoline can and a tarpaulin, ran to the truck and threw them into it. He slammed the tailgate hard shut, swung around to the drivers side, and slipped behind the wheel. Barry slammed the gearbox into reverse, spinning the tires and running the rear wheels backwards onto the sidewalk. Then he jammed it into first gear, and sped away from the poor doctor's house.

Hours before, the twosome had managed to take time at the burger joint to map out a secondary route for the Milwaukee trip, using the bike trail maps. Now Barry hurtled down one of those less traveled roads.

An hour later, Barry allowed the doctor's truck to coast into the parking lot of a fast food restaurant. He helped his companion climb out of the truck, and walked her up to and into the building.

When Barry brought two large coffees back to the table where he left Cindi, she said, "I'm sorry I'm such a baby. Some police woman I am."

Barry nodded, then added, "You probably didn't see so much of that in vice."

"Nope. Damned sure about that." Now Cindi seemed to be getting her breath back. "Barry, why would the dog bite that poor man?"

"It didn't."

"Looked like bite marks to me, Barry."

"Cindi, those bite marks were made by humans.   I think. Probably depends on your definition."

Cindi's expression didn't change.   His remarks hadn't registered. "Maybe we'll talk about this later."

"Barry, this has to do with what Father Preston said, doesn't it? What about the others? Where they in the house?"

"Louise and Lindsay were on the deck behind the dining room window. Both in about the same shape as Walter. I didn't see Father Preston. Damned if I know what this is ... I really don't have a clue.

All I know is that we'll be blamed. That I know for sure. There's another problem. This truck belongs to Doc Walt. They will be looking for it shortly. We'd best lose it soon, but I didn't want to go to the moped till you looked better."

"I'm better. I'm really not this weak, Barry. Kinda took me by surprise, I guess."

Two hours later Barry and Cindi had put the fast food joint many miles behind them. They decided to find a place to hide the truck, and then start out on the moped in the morning. They were about ten miles from the state park they planned to use when Barry saw the flasher in the rear view.

"Damn it!"

Barry pulled the truck onto the stone shoulder of the lonely back road. "It's a deputy." Now Barry reached for his luger, which he had stashed under the seat. Cindi blurted out, "What are you doing Barry?!"

"No choice Bubalouie."

"But it's broken."

Barry said nothing, and watched the deputy walk up to the truck. When he reached the half way point, Barry said "Cindi! Get out of the truck."

"Huh?"

"Get out of the truck!" Cindi opened the door, and stepped out. At the same instant, the deputy spun around on his feet, pulling his service revolver from its holster, and pointing it at Cindi. In the next split-instant, Barry flung himself hard against the door and out onto the stones, training the gun on the deputy, yelling "Drop it!" The deputy didn't drop his weapon, but instead let his arm drop straight down along his side, causing the gun to point into the stones.

The deputy cocked his head. While it was obvious to Barry that the lawman was listening to something, no radio or phone could be seen.

"Your gun is inoperable, Mr. Stewart."

"Don't think so lawman. Don't believe everything your implant has to say. I've known those things to be proven wrong. Dead wrong. I'd hate to shoot another lawman."

The deputy started to raise his weapon. "Don't do it!" Barry was agitated.

"Don't do it. Don't make me shoot you deputy. Just drop your gun, and it'll be fine. You'll go home to catch another innocent guy some other day."

"The implant is never wrong." In an old west moment, the deputy swung the barrel of his service weapon up. It was about three quarters of the way to level when Barry pulled the trigger.

Cindi's eyes widened as the ancient luger's deafening blast and the nine millimeter bullet leveled the deputy, putting him flat on his back. The deputy's gun rolled across the stones, several feet away, giving Barry just enough time to reach it with his kicking foot. His toe caught it, launching it into a high arc, and landing it about twenty feet behind the deputy's cruiser.

Now the luger was trained between the deputy's eyes. "I could see the edge of your bullet proof vest, so I guess it's your lucky day. Cindi - get some cuffs from this man's car. We'll need to slow him down."

Cindi turned to Barry, "When did you fix your gun?"

"This morning Cindi. Before the Friar got there, I used the Doc's grinder in his garage. I didn't know if my home-job firing pin would work or not. The deputy clutched his chest. "He's had the wind knocked out of him." The two ex-cops looped arms under the deputy's shoulders, dragging him to the back of his cruiser. Cindi had barely managed to clamp the cuff around the bumper before the deputy's violent twisting motion knocked her off her feet. His lunge at her was stopped short by the cuff, which yanked him down and back with awful bone crunching noises from his wrist. He pulled against the leash, his feet pushing and slipping in the stones. His face had become a contorted mask of hatred. The muscles in his upper cheeks quivered as Cindi's wide eyed look passed back to Barry. Barry's eyes matched his companion's, as he said "The Friar's video."

Cindi nodded.

"We have to go ... the deputy's backups will be here in a hell of a hurry. The twosome turned towards the truck, but the deputy's words halted them in mid step. "Barry," the deputy called out, now in a perfectly controlled manner, "Think about what's at 1189 Newton Road."

Barry stared at the lawman, who resumed his ugly face, and again began to pull violently against his cuffs.

Barry and Cindi slipped into opposite sides of the truck, and it was spitting stones before the doors were latched shut.

"We can't go far." Barry drove to the first residential drive and twisted the wheel. It was an old farmhouse, and the truck barreled first across the short drive, and then across the lawn towards the barn. "Doesn't look like anyone lives here." He drove the truck in a wide arc, turning counter-clockwise then straight up along the backside of the old building.

Twenty minutes later the twosome were on Cindi's moped running along under a power company tower easement strip, bouncing along a utility lane that was mostly tall grass and semi-rough ground.

Barry had the front portion of the seat, and Cindi clung to him as the bike moved along slowly. Barry did his best to dodge the rocks, but an occasional teeth smashing jolt brought a complaint from his passenger. Finally, the pathway smoothed out, and the speedo ticked up a little.

"Barry."

"Yeah?"

"How'd the deputy know your name?"

"Damn if I know."

"The doctor was under more scrutiny than he realized."

"That's a good bet."

"Probably bugged all to shit."

"Good bet."

"Or, it was the Friar's God machine."

Barry didn't answer.

"What was that address from the crazed deputy?"

Again, Barry didn't answer. "You recognized it?"

Barry killed the throttle of the cycle, and coasted over to the side of the pathway. "Let's talk."

They disembarked from their diminutive conveyance. Barry swept his foot sideways, dragging the kickstand into the dirt, then tested the solidity of the spot by wiggling the bike.

"Cindi, it's my mom's place."

"Your mom's place, in Milwaukee?"

"Just south of Milwaukee ... a little town ... maybe ten miles or so."

"Cindi, I think it was a death threat. They'll kill ahead of our path until they catch us, put us in the pokey, shoot us up with more neuro-toxin than Lindsay or Johnny ever got ... at the stroke of midnight."

"Yeah."

"Alicia's mom lives there too. Probably the same deal. We can't go to Milwaukee. We need to go back Cindi."

"Back where?"

"I need to talk to Kersh."

"Your old partner on the police force?"

"Yeah."

8

Flight

Two weeks later, Barry walked next to Cindi as she pushed the small cart through the parking lot of the marina. She pushed it down to the short wharf - the one for the little boats, and stopped at berth 193.

Barry boarded the boat first, and then pulled the lanyards up tight, wrapping an extra loop to steady the craft. Cindi handed him the bags, one after another, and Barry stowed them away. Cindi looked at the nomer painted artistically on the rear of the boat. "Kersh's Toy. Cute."

"Yeah - I took a big chance on Kersh. I only knew him a couple months. Sometimes ya gotta go on your gut instincts, and hope to hell you're not wrong."

"This thing big enough for ocean?"

"Not really."

"Sometimes ya gotta take a chance. Maybe we get lucky on the easy seas."

"You ever been on the ocean?"

"Nope."

The last bits to load were the three sacks of food - mostly canned and dried stuff that could be easily kept in the small supplies hold on Kersh's Toy. A stop at a clothing store had produced a very small cache of boat-wear, and another short trip to a hardware close-by to the marina had produced several sun shielding tarpaulins. "Kersh's Toy" had not been designed for week long ocean voyages, and its defense against the relentless gulf reflected sun would have been less than inadequate. Barry turned to Cindi, "Hey gorgeous, are you ready to die?"

"Guess so. How long do we need to be lucky in order to ... you know ... not die?"

"About a week, plus or minus. Kersh is an inter-waterway fisherman, so he had the extra tanks built in. We've got about ninety gallons of fuel. My math says that it's possible that'll be enough. Barely."

"Possible?"

"Yup. Depends on the weather. We'll have to run the motor in rough seas just to keep the water out, and in rough seas we'll get nowhere fast. We really need some flat water. Do you know of any seafarer goddesses we can pray to?"

An hour and a half later, the dim outline of the shore faded completely away. "Here goes nothing."

"Hey Barry - where's the optimism?"

"Ahead of us. I'm hoping." Barry pointed out at the gulf, which was flat as a pancake, while the motor churned in the blue water and pushed the little craft forward, leaving only a small wake in its path.

Barry pointed at the throttle. "We'll run about half speed for the best mileage. Or is that knotage?"

"Some seafarer."

"Yeah. Hope the seat of my pants hold up."

Cindi laughed, "So I see you have some real fancy seat of the pants navigation equipment there." Cindi pointed at the compass that Barry had purchased at the hardware. The fancy electronic equipment, built into the main console next to the rudder wheel, was dark and blank. "Kersh warned me not to use the on-board electronics. It's too new-fangled, and uses some kind of continuous built-in communication link to contact navigation markers, beacons, and so forth. The link would send alerts to close-by coast guard cutters, giving them info about our presence. The boat license ID is tagged into the transponder, and would indicate the size of the boat, and the clear fact that the mad sailors on Kersh's Toy could only be in these dark waters in order to commit suicide. They'd be on us in a short while."

"Mad, mad sailors."

"The route we are taking is even more insane Cindi."

"How so?"

"I'm staying out of the sea-lanes, because any freighter captain would have the same reaction as the cutter crew. We can't be seen. Staying out of the sea lanes keeps the probability of that lower. There are the high altitude drug smuggler surveillance planes, but our slow speed and size helps against that. So, in one way our route is pretty good."

"And in the other way?"

"In all other ways, our plan represents a suicidal urge. If the seas get rough, we'll be very unlikely to be rescued - assuming we really wanted to be. I think we'll not fire any flares, given how it is ... so I guess it doesn't matter very much."

Barry continued, "The boat is too short for the wavelength of the ocean when it's angry. If the worst happens, we'll turn headlong into the swells and keep the motor running flat out. I think that seas much over ten feet will do us in pretty quickly. Kersh had just started to explain that part when I cut him off. I didn't really want to know."

Two days passed, and the seas remained flat as a board. Barry rigged the tarpaulins to cover about half the boat, and the seafaring twosome rested under them, trying to avoid the almost inevitable sunburns. Barry mentioned at one point that "The gulf reflection gets us almost as well as the overhead ... especially with the good weather." He was pretty sure that when the two of them finally made landfall, they would resemble landlubber beach lobsters."

By the third evening, Cindi and Barry had talked out most of the easy stuff. Dinnertime found them looking at each other, while munching on cardboard quality vending machine fare from the hold.

"Why did you take me with you, Barry?"

"Couldn't leave you."

"Why not?"

Barry smiled, picked up the other half of his peanut-buttered cracker, and tossed it into his mouth. He kept on with his fixed grin for a long while, then said, "I didn't know what to do, so I went with what was already lined up. Less decision work that way."

"Don't use that line in a bar Barry."

"I hung onto a mental image that I had of Alicia and myself, and our relationship, for years. We once had something pretty good, and I just always kept that fixed picture-perfect fantasy in my mind. It was the only way it could be, and I couldn't make any decision to have it any other way. I wanted it back, and so I just decided to keep treading water - no matter if I drowned or not."

"Then, I made the decision to run. I guess, maybe, all along I was looking for a rationalization to do it. Finally, when it looked like Alicia could be hurt, I jumped on that as a rationalization, and-"

"And?"

"Here we are."

Barry looked at Cindi. She was stretched over the top of the smallest storage hold on Kersh's Toy, one that now took the secondary purpose of being a half-sized waterproof sofa. That small section of fiberglass and nylon boat fabric now served to support Cindi's beautiful bikini clad body. Barry found himself entranced, unashamedly drawing her into his eyes, taking in the soft slopes of her feminine form, oblivious to any usual or expected socially engendered restraints, losing suddenly all conscious holds on himself and his feelings. The shield dropped away from his facial expression, and he became as transparent as the gulf waters slowly swirling around Kersh's Toy.

Day Four

The dawn had not yet come, but Barry was jostled awake by the pounding of the waves against the hull. Opening his eyes, he saw Cindi standing at the wheel. He could see that she had donned the thin plastic parka that was a cheap-rack find at the hardware. Now it fluttered in the breeze that, Barry thought, was at least ten degrees cooler than when he went to sleep, and much stronger. "It's picking up."

"Yeah. You never did give me any seafaring goddess prayers darling."

"Waves are only a few feet, but the air has a nasty feeling that I'm not liking very much Barry." Barry flipped open the lid on the small hold, and grabbed his cheap-rack rain gear, pushing his arms into it. He moved up to Cindi, and put his arm around her. "Guess I can take the wheel for a while ... give you a break."

Thirty minutes later, the swells were at six or seven feet, and the little boat began to live up to its name, rocking like a little toy in a too-big tub. The sea water came over from the bow and stern, port and lee sides. It seemed to be coming from every direction at once. The gulf water had been warm, but now the wind driven spray seemed icy cold.

Cindi pulled Barry's hood away from his ear, and put her mouth inside of it. "How about Aphrodite? Didn't she have something to do with the ocean?" Barry laughed over the din of the wind, "Yeah, but that one had a very bad ending. Something about Zeus having a very bad day, if I remember correctly."

Cindi pulled the thin, wet plastic back again, shouting "Hey Zeus."

"Very funny, but better prayer."

Now the bow was taking water on every wave. Barry exclaimed, "The boat's too damned short - just like Kersh said!" Cindi's only response was to pull him in more tightly. Barry looked back to the large hold area adjacent to the engine compartment. About a foot of water had collected there, and he jumped back to the stern, pulling on the engine cover grip, and dropping his head down into the compartment. He poked his head out, yelling up to Cindi, "Bilge is running - it just can't keep up!" He wasn't sure she had heard him over the wind, which now seemed like an all-out gale to Barry. Barry had never been in a gale, full blown or not, but as far as he was concerned, as of this moment, he qualified as gale experienced. When he returned to the wheel stoop, Cindi saw that he carried a rolled rope. He began to tie a loop around Cindi, and then one around himself. The other ends, he clipped onto a wheelhouse support that seemed sturdy and was welded onto the deck. "At least we'll go down with the boat."

"Real capitan-like Barry. Chivalrous."

"Aren't you supposed to save the women and children?"

"You know something Cindi, you sure don't take this whole dying in a gale in the middle of the gulf thing very seriously."

"We ain't dying Bubualouie!"

Neither of the young lovers saw it coming. Their only warning was a sudden lifting sensation - pushing up on the bottoms of their shoes, like a triple speed elevator ... like a carnival ride gone wrong. The elevator slipped out from under them, making them weightless and horizontal, but only for the moment it took for the rope to fully extend. Then the sudden tightening of the ropes caused the carnival ride to have a wrench thrown into its works, jerking the twosome painfully in the opposite direction - back away from where the wave had thrown them. The unintended action of the rope was to slam both their bodies hard against the deck. Neither had the sense to know what was happening, but both were vaguely cognizant of the fact that they were hanging by the ropes, upside down. Kersh's Toy hung in space, its bow pointing straight up at the darkness that would normally have been blue sky - but only for the sort of moment the roller coaster rider experiences as up turns to down. The boat came crashing down again, miraculously remaining upright. It had not capsized, but it had taken water.

The wind stopped before either of the newly experienced seafarers had completely regained their wits or taken inventory of their damages. It was as if the gale had given them its best, but now was beaten. It retreated more quickly than it came. Two hours later, the tired and bruised lovers recuperated, lying in a boat that rocked slowly, the waves nipping so lightly that it it could have all been a very bad dream. A bad dream, excepting for the fact that they were both bleeding from the mouth. Barry was missing a tooth, and Cindi had a loose one. Cindi's "Hey, I could pull mine out so we match," finally made them laugh again, and decide that yes – they were still alive.

Day five returned to the flat sea normalcy that had spoiled them at the beginning of their voyage.

On the eighth day, Kersh's Toy floated into the sleepy fisherman's marina that Kersh had suggested as the most low profile and low risk. The trip had changed Cindi and Barry's race, morphing them from caucasian Northerners into what, for anything that the fishermen standing next to the berth might think with only a quick look, were two Latino lovers. The twosome disembarked the boat, and walked hand in hand up to the marina's gate and its only building.

The illegal immigrants had purposely made landfall at the isolated fisherman's wharf. Kersh had been clear about the risk, and told them exactly where to go. He told Barry, "Costa Rica doesn't have the world's largest navy or coast guard. You should be OK. Then - look up my people."

It was Kersh's people that Barry sought now. Having only rudimentary police force on-the-job Spanish language skills made things challenging, to say the least.

The two port guard officials looked across at Barry and Cindi as they walked up to the gate. Barry's limited Spanish was good enough to understand the conversation between the two of them. Basically, "They couldn't have come from anyplace else in that boat." "No problem."

The documents supplied by Kersh worked flawlessly. Soon, Barry and Cindi were making their way through the fishing port village.

Months later, Cindi and Barry sat on the deck overlooking the coffee fields. Their hosts had spared nothing to make them comfortable. Cindi asked, "You think things will ever change so that we can go back?"

Barry looked at her, lovingly. "I don't know darling. I really don't know. Good coffee."

"Just roasted this morning sweetie."

Barry smiled, and raised his cup.

A Few Reflections

W rite what is in your heart, so long as you understand that it is good. Pray ye that it is good, and not evil, so that it brings the light and not the darkness of the draught that would extinguish it.

The Drug

The Drug

Copyright Ronald Lee Scheckelhoff 2011

Art graciously provided by the waters of
Jordan Lake, in North Carolina

Author/Publisher DBA:

Kristen's Tree Publishing

(Distributor for trade shows & book fairs)

First Release Printing (SE)

(novelette version)

Sept 28th, 2011

1

Miguel/Jorge

T wice. It had happened twice before, but Miguel was still willing to put it off as chance. He stared down at his Seven Layer salad – or what was left of it, and wished there were a little more to eat. The twelve ounce package from the Deli was only a dollar more, but Miguel's instinct for spending money slowly stayed with him always. It kept him thin.

Miguel was a product of Mexico's university system, and he had managed to land a position and a pretty nice salary in the States when he immigrated only two years before. It's not that his Mexican university credentials were likely to impress the people at companies like Kesos Technology Corp, but it *did* help a great deal that the founder was a Mexican immigrant himself.

Miguel's style and personality helped a bit too. With his high pitched boyish voice and the excited, enthusiastic cadence of his speech and mannerisms, he soon won over the interviewer at Kesos, who was *not* of Mexican descent.

Miguel finished the salad and tossed the container into the company trash can. Not one for tactful humor, the plant superintendent had painted letters on the side of the can. The artfully brushed letters advised: "Your trash goes here or your job does." Apparently, the management was fed up with taking care of other people's trash. "Doesn't really match the tenor of the place," mused Miguel. Even the superintendent was a real nice guy as far as he knew.

As Miguel started back towards the patio lunchroom door, he took another look over his shoulder – at the scene that had engrossed him throughout most of his lunch. "Coincidence," he thought. "Yeah – there's some other explanation for it."

Back inside the building, Miguel found his last set of diagrams spread out across his desk. They were horribly marked up with red ink – as if the school marm grammar teacher had gone berserk while wielding a red pen and a vengeance for grammatical correctness taken to it most anal extension.

Miguel smiled. Miguel had recognized that his boss was taken with micro management from day one at Kesos. Regardless of that fact, Stan had consistently recognized Miguel's talents in a way that sometimes irritated the other employees in Stan's group. On the last page, a big red circle surrounded the words "Great job Miguel!" Just below the emblazoned compliment was written "It just needs a little more work."

Jorge

Jorge was nearing the end of the shift. "Man – has it been a long day or what?" he asked himself. He was eager for the last hour to end. The construction crew managers had all seemed so happy to see him when he applied for the position three weeks earlier. They said things like "you'll fit right in," and "you'll be a pro in no time at all." Subsequently, he found that the work was more physically demanding than he had thought it would be. Jorge didn't carry the build of a linebacker, but he was no pencil geek, by a long stretch. He grew up in a crime infested part of Mexico – for the most part overrun by drug cartel muscle men and their assortment of sordid assassins. He had managed – he thought – to save his skin on one occasion, only by being stronger than the two others involved in the fracas, one of whom was killed (ironically, by his co-assassin).

Jorge was young and without a great deal of experience in the construction industry. He had done a stint at a local poultry factory that didn't work out well, and so he applied for the construction job that offered a little more money. Still, the rate of pay was not very great. It was nothing like Miguel's. Something else not shared with Miguel was Jorge's legal status. Unlike Miguel, Jorge was an illegal.

Jorge had friends – people he knew – people he stayed with. Most of them were illegal too. He had some citizen friends, and even some non-hispanic ones. One of them, Curtis, had advised Jorge that he was lucky. As an explanation, he told Jorge, "The major portion of the hassle the government can lay on you comes because you are a numbered citizen. It makes it a simple matter to find you." Curtis believed that Jorge had an advantage in many ways, because Jorge was unnumbered, and in many ways - non-existent.

Jorge didn't believe it – not for a minute. His life had been hassle enough, number or no number. Also, Jorge's handlers always seemed to know where he was anyway. It was an uncanny, even creepy idea, and Jorge felt a growing paranoia about the people who, in the beginning, had been so helpful.

The Mexicans dropped their belts and tools into the bins. Eddie made sure they dropped everything, and waved them towards the gate. Eddie was creepy, but nothing compared to Jimmy.

Jimmy was the creepiest of the handlers. He was the *always smiling man.* No matter what he did or said, Jimmy was smiling like a fool. If it ever turned out that the 2012 cult people really did have the right ticket, then on the prophesied night when the hurtling fireball of death could be seen big and red in the sky - there would be Jimmy. Phony Jimmy would be there alright, and he'd be smiling. "He'd be showing his big teeth, that's for sure," Jorge thought as he moved out of the gate next to the corner shack in the stone yard where Jimmy kept shop.

Catching Jorge's eye, the toothy one gave his best impression of the *White Brite* commercial advertisement as Jorge moved through the gate. "You stay out of trouble now Jorge!" Jorge nodded and walked past Jimmy, and out into the parking lot to find the crew's taxi of the week, Justo's old Civic. As the noisy old wreck finally fired with an accompanying cackle from the muffler, Jorge reprimanded Justo, "Damn, when are you going to fix this old thing?"

2

The Apartment

He awakened from his reverie slowly – fighting it – resisting the moment of awareness that he knew would destroy the fantasy – the one that lived in his slumber. Sharply, the light from the window sliced away the last vestigial shred of unconsciousness. His eyes opened, and dimly focused upon the round form of the stool beneath his feet. Shoving it away from himself, he rose from the chair, disgusted that his own lonely life had returned to haunt him. "I make love with a fiction of my own mind," became his first internally verbalized thought.

Miguel walked to the window, and looked out of it. She was real enough, of course. She was as real as flesh and blood could make her. But, she lived in another life, far away from his, and separated by the chasm of a thousand years. He pulled a piece of day old toast from the toaster, first removing a piece of broken plastic that obstructed it. He used everything until it was broken beyond repair, to the point of its having lost all function, and even then he found another use for it. He shoved the stiff piece of bread back into the thing, and pushed down on the lever. After a couple firefly sparks across the bottom and within the innards of the old appliance, its coils glowed again and in a moment resurrected his breakfast from its cold death.

"I'm not in love," he told himself, "It's just not the same – love and appreciation. I can appreciate such beauty as she has, and not be in love, can't I?"

Miguel moved to the window on the other side of the apartment. Standing there, the physical mass of his being pressed down upon the furnace grating under his toes, making small sounds as he rocked in place. He looked at the car – the familiar one that was always parked in that place at a point on the end of his gaze.

It was *her* car, and she was home in her apartment just now, across the street and one door down. He had tried to notice her schedule, but it was impossible. There was no rhythm or rhyme to it, and in any case he felt guilty for thinking so much about that spot on the street, and always wondering whether or not it was filled. Can a man stalk with his eyes, from a hidden place, watching what no one knows he watches? Miguel stopped rocking when a drip of hot coffee dribbled over the top of his too-full cup and onto his toes, awaking him from his reverie. He shuffled over to the fireplace, grabbed a stoker, and prodded the coals. "God, I hate January," he half mumbled to himself ...

Domingo

"Just as soon as you give me the money Jorge!" Pulling into the space next to the apartment, Justo twisted the key and silenced the noisy Civic. The first three of them loitered under the barren tree next to the parking lot, each making use of Justo's shared package of cigarettes, as Domingo went into the apartment to turn on the heat.

Domingo and Jorge came from villages close to each other in Mexico, and realized this fact after their association was made to rent the apartment ... something that resulted, naturally enough, from their common workplace. As illegals, they moved frequently, and their requirement for new accommodations was handled easily by the new job – and by Jimmy's convenient *referral*. Justo had been with Jimmy and his bosses for awhile, and was the original tenant of the rooms. Peter, the other member of the carpool, had not taken a room with them, but usually shared some after hours talk, relaxation and maybe a beverage or two before walking back to his nearby apartment.

Domingo pulled some chips down from the cupboards, and tossed them onto the counter. He took some cheese dip from the fridge, and put it out. As the other three came into the room, he quipped "How's that for table service?" Peter grabbed a handful and sauntered over to the largest and most beat-up of the half upholstered chairs, plopping down into it. Twice the size of any of the others, he required the extra space. Domingo took the skinny chair. His frail form made sharp contrast with Peter's, and he seemed an odd fellow to work the construction trade. He was an expert cabinet maker and millwright, doing every day those things that took a little more in the way of a sharp eye and the correct measure of natural patience. He was also the most easy going of the group, and that was probably for the same reason.

Domingo had religion, and that was another juxtaposition of an unlikely construction worker attribute onto the slender body just as unlikely to be there. His coworkers, if they had known the correct verse in Romans, by Apostle Paul, would not have chided him for saying the prayers around the occasional group meal, and simultaneously for being a hypocrite. None of these men imagined any divine right of authority in the government they every day feared and avoided. Jorge remembered what Domingo had said about the Romans verse being misused and misquoted frequently, saying "Paul himself was a rebel for half his life, and especially so because he was a former centurion and thus a traitor in the eyes of the Romans."

It didn't help that the most immediate form of authority that they all submitted to – the construction bosses – often mistreated them. Domingo usually defended his Anglo friends when making such references to authority, because he had occasion to work for folks who did not abuse him. About his current bosses he carefully avoided comment. "Walls have ears around here," he once said to Jorge.

Jorge and Domingo spent more time in conversation with each other than with the others, and this was quite natural as they were the newcomers. Jorge had been for a time keenly aware of spooky omens - feelings that seemed to imply to him an unseen oversight. Although he could not put his finger on a reason, the two originals of the quintet seemed to present a vague association with those feelings. Domingo seemed safer, both because of his relative newness and the prayer book's tattered corner that always protruded from the religious man's rear pocket.

Jorge's thoughts were that some men speak religion, and some live it. Domingo was one to live it. The man had nary a bad word to say, even to his antagonists, although the treatment he received from the company handlers sometimes irritated him. It was then that he would grab his prayerbook to find a form of reconciliation and recourse. "The antagonist's best weapon is his victim's own anger" he had said to Jorge once, when in the beginning, Jorge made his novice blunders and the supervisors berated him. It was funny, but subsequently, when he encountered similar situations, he could just look at Domingo and feel better about it. Sometimes Domingo could see him doing this, and would smile and nod.

Jorge had the idea that the man should have been a padre. He wondered a little bit, why he was not.

3

February

He was standing in his favorite spot, and the hot air rushing through the waffles in the iron grate warmed his feet through his socks. Although the parking space was empty, Miguel's gaze was tightly fixed into a mindless stare. In a blur, the familiar vehicle filled the spot, its unusual color of wine hued charcoal fading in as the jagged yellow lines below it faded out. The door opened, and the familiar form appeared - a form flowing inside of a dress too loose and summery for February. The wind caught it briefly as she stood upright, her statuesque body holding the fabric as it flapped behind her, like a flag flying away from its mooring on a windy day.

Likewise, as she turned, the tufts of her hair followed the wind, which blew all semblance of order from them. "Where is your coat," thought Miguel, "... on such a blustery day?!" Swiftly, she spun around to the rear door of the car, and opened it. She reached down to pick up a tightly bound wrapping of papers. Stuffing it firmly under her arm, she hustled off in the direction of her apartment door.

She wasn't a complete stranger to Miguel, and he had made some small conversation with her using the pretext of leaving the apartment in *his* car, which he parked, not coincidentally, behind hers. Miguel was an odd composite of nature - he had extraordinary good looks in combination with just as an extraordinary volume of shyness. He naturally attracted women to him, based upon his looks, but his difficulty lay in connecting with the ones who *attracted him*. Such was the paradox of his young life. He sat in his apartment and calculated how he might establish something more than a "passing in the parking spaces" kind of affair.

She was a thousand miles away from him by being, probably, the better part of twice his age ... a sophisticated woman not likely impressed by his boyish naivety.

Yet, his desire to meet her on some socially compatible level had become overpowering. He loved her now, only in his dream powered proxy, slipping into her arms almost every night, and awakening only to the sad realization of what remained an unaccomplished mission.

Miguel put his coffee cup in the dishwasher, grabbed his briefcase, and whisked himself out to his car. Occasionally it was this way in the mornings, with her returning to her place just as he began his new day.

The Police Call

Stan was waiting for Miguel when he slipped into his office cubicle with fifteen minutes to spare. Stan's arms were crossed.

"Miguel. What the hell is going on? You called the cops yesterday afternoon, didn't you?" Miguel was instantly embarrassed. He began "Wha- " but Stan cut him off. "You used the company cell phone to make the call, Miguel. The vice president of operations got a call from the police, and he is mad as hell. Why did you report those people, and what kind of crazy story did you tell the police dispatcher? And why?"

Miguel took a deep breath, and started out "I thought it was all just my imagination the first time Stan. Really, I didn't report anything the first time, but this time I just felt something was funny about it." Stan looked at Miguel, and the steam subsided. He knew his star engineer was not of the nature to send the police out on a wild goose chase.

Miguel always seemed confidently in control of himself, and was a logic driven fellow. Stan put it to his charge, "Miguel. Neither George nor myself could contemplate why the project foreman you accused would do such a thing to his crew. Just seemed silly, you know. Their operations manager called ours, George Whitehall, and basically threatened a lawsuit." Miguel looked sheepish. "But," continued Stan, "George confided that he thinks it's not likely they will, it's not something they will consider worth following. George was angry though, very angry, and he asked me to convey that to you. Don't make any more calls Miguel. None. Unless your calls are in direct reference to chemical engineering, don't make them." "OK?"

Miguel shook his head in the affirmative, as he turned to leave.

Valerie

The roll of papers separated as it hit the pavement, scattering around the street, soon hopelessly lost in the wind. Miguel was positioned, entirely by coincidence this time, to be nearly close enough to intervene as she fell into the street gutter. "My papers!" she exclaimed as she rolled over onto the street, dropping her face into her hands as she watched them all flitter away. The breeze was strong and there was no hope of chasing and collecting them. Instinctively, Miguel reached down to help her to her feet. As she regained her balance, she tottered slightly, and used her hand and Miguel's shoulder to steady herself. Miguel said "You're not hurt, Miss?" After putting some weight on the turned ankle, she responded with "I think I'm OK," and then, "my high heel twisted on a stone or something, I think. I hate these things."

"By the way, my name is Valerie. Friends like to call me Val, but I really prefer Valerie." She half held out her hand ... "And you are?" "Miguel. No nickname, really ... just Miguel." She studied him. "Nice name," she continued. Miguel had been looking out into the distance, avoiding her eyes, but just now their two gazes locked briefly. Smiling eyes, he thought, but he broke the connection. The moment was a little more than he had bargained for, and his shy demeanor began to take control.

His one sided fantasy had gone too far, making him a secret voyeur, and for this he felt embarrassed ... even ashamed. Feeling the need to keep the match from the striker, he kept averting her look. "Be cool," he thought. He reminded himself that he was far ahead of her in this race for which she had taken no number.

Valerie took one last look in the direction of the wind and her lost work, turned and shrugged at Miguel. "Nice meeting you," she said, and headed off in the direction of her apartment door.

The Crew

Jorge and Domingo had been assigned to work crew B, and slowly they became familiar with stories told by the others in the crew – about each other's backgrounds, families, and often about the troubles surrounding their individual paths to illegal immigration.

The "crew" was really making a stinking mess of things, and the foremen were now starting to express displeasure with the whole lot of them. Between themselves, they talked about it.

Excepting for Domingo, every one of crew B was a neophyte, thrown to the wolves and making mistakes at every turn. The entire east wall of the project had to be torn down and rebuilt – much to the dismay of the project leader – who didn't think it was possible to screw up that badly. Eddie was the project leader for the fiasco, and because he was responsible for the mess, had recently been putting some heat on the foremen to shape the men into some kind of team that could go forward more than backward. Peter and Justo were experienced, but they were not members of *work crew B*. Feelings related to low job performance and the loss of job security became a target of conversation and a generator of pressure.

This pressure was brought back to apartment number *1032* every night, where Peter and Justo rolled eyes at each other and pretended to be empathetic to the stories. Occasionally Peter could be heard to make a suggestion that was worthwhile, but Justo usually just nodded. He might say "It'll come with time. Be happy. Be patient."

During the infrequent times that Domingo and Jorge found themselves alone – they talked about it, and how it made no sense. "Why would they not put some experienced people in with us, for cry'in out loud" was a lament proffered more than once by Jorge. From Domingo came a different lament.

"They're really not using my talents anyway. I mean, I'm a wood worker – not a cement mixer and water boy."

Oktoberfest

It was Saturday, the eleventh.   Miguel had nothing in particular on his mind that he felt obligated to do.   He jumped into his Volvo, which was his habit when he had nothing in particular to do.   On the corner of the street leading out from the cul-de-sac where he lived, he saw the accordion player and the big signs, could hear the *really* old world music, and the tent where – almost certainly – he might find something to do. It seemed odd to have an Oktoberfest when it was *not October*, but Miguel remembered that the Germans were always the ones looking for an excuse.   It was a little after two o'clock, and he had not yet taken his lunch.   The bratwurst was convenient for this – and he sat down in the shade of the tent, at a table near the rear of it, because the accordion player had his amplifier turned up a notch or two too high. Miguel munched on his sandwich, wincing a little at the strong kraut on it, and nodding his head to the music.   Polka – it was the really old world stuff that reminded him of home.   Thinking about it, he decided that the traditional Mexican music was not far removed from it, in some sort of not-quite-identifiable way. Really, a lot of it *is polka*, he mused, but without Bavarian garments and with different beer.   And the kraut.   Wincing again, "Man, what was I thinking?"

Next to the amplifier stand was a table not far back from the lowest row of speakers. A woman sat there, facing away from him.   Thinking that the woman was very familiar in some way, he noticed the cut of her dress. His mental imagery told him that it was familiar, and then it hit him all at once.

The woman was Valerie! "What to do?" seemed like a voice in his head, and it was immediately followed by "Stop being a shy little schmuck, you asshole."   Casting his nature aside, suddenly being the brave one, he walked up to the table and placed his cup of Heineken next to Valerie's. Valerie jumped a little, as the loud blast from the speakers covered Miguel's approach. Immediately, her surprise was followed by a smile and nod when Miguel asked, "May I?"

The two figures sat at the table for a long time, and while certainly the talk was mostly small, the accordion player's amplifier worked stupendously in Miguel's favor – forcing the conversation to happen with cupped hands very close to ears. Just how beneficial that accordion player's music might be, Miguel soon would learn.

4

March

Miguel was breathless. His breathing slowed as the first rays of consciousness poked him unsoftly, and began to levitate him from his slumber. For a few moments, his feelings spun through the familiar territory, but in the fog of his slow awakening, in the manner of his habit and his every morning, he thought of the woman. He was abruptly aware now, that his hand rested upon the gentle slope of the womanly form next to him. "No," he smiled to himself, "it was no longer fantasy." Miguel considered his happy situation, and how his long, careful plan had been taken to fruition.

Miguel thought about his actuated love, and the woman whose name was a nearly a movie. Valerie Star was her name, she had told him. He thought about what had transpired in only six weeks span of time, and how they each, in their own way, finally admitted that they were in love. At some point, this awareness became firm, and then it remained only to wait for the timely spark, and the moment that would consume them both and that they would not resist.

In the beginning, she had dazzled him with her weapons – those womanly attributes that every woman keeps at the ready. Like all men, in the beginning Miguel misunderstood her use of them, and as is often the case, she felt let down by his attraction to them. The paradox is clear, and it played out in the beginning of their relationship. Always, it is the woman who chooses.

The rules of the old game have never changed, and the woman must always guard suspiciously against her intended's falling for those things she has brought to bear, and not for the hand that bears them. Valerie's weapons had done their work well, and Miguel had been slain.

Peterson

Peterson's voice waffled across the top of the cubicle wall. Miguel tossed his coat onto the extra chair in his own space. Pushing his own chair to the opening and sitting in it, he cocked his ear, watching the corner office discretely.

Stan stood at the dry erase board that stretched all along the far wall of the room. Instantly, Miguel recognized the scrawl to which Stan now pointed as a portion of his own process diagram. Peterson pointed to it, asking a question that was too muffled by the glass partition to hear very clearly. Miguel saw that it was the same part of the document that had attracted Stan's red flowing marker pen. Miguel looked confused now, not understanding the meaning behind the lines of chalk. Something had been added to the diagram. Sketched into the corner and highlighted with a big caret sign was an extra cooling unit. "That is downright strange," thought Miguel, "because the reaction doesn't require it, and in fact is barely exothermic. What the hell?"

Now Miguel noticed another modification – an additional reactant vessel had been plumbed into the part of the diagram containing the CSTR reactor. Miguel's mind wandered. "Why is Stan taking over my project? Why doesn't he just ask me to do it?" Miguel felt hurt because, apparently, Stan didn't trust him. Shaking his head, he mumbled "It's ridiculous, the reaction is simple enough that any first year student write it up."

Q
uirks

Valerie stepped out of the kitchen as Miguel entered his own apartment. Valerie looked unhappy. In the time they had spent together, Miguel had learned the little quirks of her personality, and some were hard to deal with.

Often she presented with a facade of sternness and a stiff upper lip, all the while exuding an underlying telepathy that invited the melting of it. Once again confronted with this paradox, Miguel thought of an icebreaker. "C'mon Valerie, don't look so frumpy. Let me take you out to a real nice restaurant. We'll have some dinner ... your favorites ... how about it? I have something I want to run by you – stuff at work that I'm not too happy about. I need to borrow your shoulder, maybe." Miguel thought he saw just a hint of a smile in Valerie's eyes, but the corner of her mouth curled up only a little bit. The change was barely perceptible. "OK," she responded.

Miguel opened the car door for Valerie. That really old school stuff made her feel special, new world or not. She slid onto the seat of the Volvo. Soon, Miguel was merging into the late evening traffic on the boulevard. Moving down it and then across the midtown bridge – about five miles altogether –

Miguel said nothing. Valerie reopened the conversation, "Something's bugging you, sweetheart. You can have my shoulder now."

"Yeah, it's weird ... what's been going on there. A while back I called the police for something, and my superiors went completely crazy over it. I'm getting bad vibes lately." At dinner, it was Valerie who said not a thing. Miguel poured his frustrations out on his lover, and she quietly took it all in. "Valerie." "You're still looking frumpy and you've had your favorite meal. C'mon ... what's bugging *you*?" A hint of sadness flashed across her face and disappeared. "Well, Miguel ..." Miguel cut her off, "Are you pregnant?!" "No, Miguel, it's not that. No, not at all. You know, it's just my biorhythm that's out of kilter or something. Hasn't that ever happened to you?"

Miguel took in her response, "OK. Well, what do you think about my work. Does it sound like I should be worried?" Valerie smiled for the first time in the evening, though it seemed to Miguel that she was making an effort for it. "I think you should just forget about the whole thing, Miguel. Stan gave you another project to work on, right? There's probably a good reason he wants to farm out the rest of the other project. Hey – you're the one whose always saying that you like variety. Just put it out of your mind."

Miguel thought about it. Valerie rejoined, "Anyway, if Stan had problems with you he wouldn't give you an even bigger project, right?" Miguel shrugged. "You're the smart one at this table. Thanks for that shoulder."

Wrong Address

When Domingo walked into the room, it was late. Justo sat at the table, looking at a Spanish language newspaper. Domingo pulled his shoulders up squarely and looked at Justo, "You're the night owl tonight Justo!" "Ah, I couldn't sleep, that's all." Justo measured Domingo, looking at him in a way that seemed to belie an unasked question. Domingo found his demeanor odd, but nodded. "I'm going to bed."

It was five in the morning when Domingo slipped out of the apartment door. Being Saturday, the crew was idle, and all of Domingo's apartment mates were making good use of their bedsteads to catch up on the just finished week.

Domingo had been careful to park the beat up old Nissan in the adjacent lot away from the rooms where his roommates now slept. He shook the cobwebs out of his head. Working on two hours of sleep was going to be unpleasant, but he had to have his answer. The little four cylinder groaned slightly, then cackled, driving into Domingo's feet those familiar vibrations of a car driven far past its design mileage limit. Domingo pulled out on the street. Driving a few blocks, he twisted the wheel and pulled across the midtown bridge.

It was a thirty minute run out to the place Domingo sought. The address, he had scribbled into a little notepad – the one he always carried with him and (*when he was actually doing what he was good at*) he used in his work. The decrepit car's brakes slowed it to a roll at a specific point on the road. Domingo looked about himself. Finally, he pulled onto the berm and killed the engine.

On his side of the road, Domingo saw an expanse of space leading back to an old junk yard. On the other lie a small lagoon - and situated next to it an abandoned utility trailer, used for some long forgotten purpose. Domingo pulled the notepad from his pocket, and scrutinized the address. "Makes no sense at all," he thought. "Where the hell is it?" Shaking his head once more – on one level to express his disbelief and another to remove the cobwebs that had crept in again – he walked back to the car.

Peter was there when Domingo returned to the apartment. Domingo nodded to the man he never appreciated much. "No work today Peter. Looking for breakfast?" "Where's Jorge?" The big man rose from his designated chair, and moved towards Domingo. "They went away on a little errand," came from the big man, now hulking before the frail one. "What's the prob-" Domingo almost voiced the words, but not quite. Peter's giant hands were around the slender man's neck and pushing him backwards at the same time.

A one-time football player and now brutal enforcer, Peter's two hundred eighty pounds of muscle pushed Domingo's neck backwards and down into the sink he had been crushed up against ...

Miguel, my Love

The lovers hurried into the apartment. Barely had they crossed the threshold before the urgency of their plan overtook them, and they ripped at each other's garments ... the frustrations in both of them, different but pressing, required release, and they took it. Madly, they took it. Valerie closed her eyes and threw herself into her escape, attempting and succeeding, if only for a short time, a remission from all of the melancholy knowledge she carried, the knowledge that tore at her soul and brought darkness to her brightest days. "I love you," she mouthed, again and again.

The morning saw a rare smile on Valerie's face. Still, Miguel mused, she hadn't shaken her biorhythm kilter problem. But she was better. She sat across from Miguel at the table.

Being Saturday, the twosome could claim the whole day for themselves, and they were both looking forward to it. They made it a lazy time, with neither of them thinking much about anything outside of each other. They reveled in the hours, as only two lovers can ever do, making a celebration of all the mundane things that they did, like shopping for Miguel's extra work shirts. Valerie did not say much, other than with her eyes. Other than when she received the gaze of Miguel's eyes into her own, the shadows always returned to them.

Monday Morning

On Monday morning Justo and Jorge jumped into the Civic at six fifteen, already fifteen minutes past the time they could afford to wait and not be late for work. "Wonder what happened to them," said Jorge. "Damned if I know," returned Justo. "It's just not like Peter to drop out like that. I don't know about your friend Domingo." Jorge paused a second, "Well, I don't really know him either."

"You and Domingo seem to talk more than anybody." Jorge breathed out a sigh, "It's a little weird, I'll admit, but even though I have only known him a short while, this is cause for concern. Someone ought to call the police, even though it's two grown men who should be able to take care of themselves. Especially Peter. Who the hell would mess with him?" Justo grinned. Yeah, have you ever seen him lifting the heavy lumber? The man's a beast, that's for sure. You're right. Nobody would mess with him. But – the police? They aren't gonna look for man with a bogus ID Jorge."

Jimmy was yelling at them when they pulled into the lot next to the stone yard. "Where have you boys been? You're late, damn it, and you're not pretty enough to make me wait." "Puleeese get your gear from your bins and meet me at the truck. Pronto! Justo! You're working *B Crew* today!"

News

The police cruiser moved slowly along the frontage of the construction site, and a collective but barely discernible sigh of anxiety passed through the crew. The officer was met on the grassy area along the roadway in an area not yet outfitted with a sidewalk - by the honcho of the day, a Mr. RM Johnson. The voices of the two men shifted back and forth for a few minutes. The officer turned and walked back to a place behind the cruiser, and then popped open the trunk. He motioned for Johnson to walk back to him. Reaching down into the car, the officer fetched an evidence bag. From it he retrieved a construction company shirt – part of a uniform.

The distant crew could not see that it was horribly bloodied, or that amid the splatters a name tag was visible, sewn into the fabric. They could not see that the front of it was slit a dozen times. "Apparently," began the officer, "this man's name was Domingo." "Why are you showing this to me?" queried Johnson. The officer continued, "We found a car with plates on it that were registered to your construction company, Mr. Johnson. It had been pushed down to the water's edge, near the midtown bridge, about half a block downstream. Someone had done a very poor job of hiding it under some scrub brush and small tree limbs."

"There were two sets of tracks leading to the water, down in an area where the slosh from the boats keeps the ground wet. Only one set of tracks returned. Is this man your employee?"

Johnson thought a moment, and hesitated. "It does look like one of our shirts, and we *do* have an employee who goes by that name. Also, a man by that name did not report for work, so I suppose it could be him." The officer traded questions and answers with Johnson for a few more minutes, and then returned to his car. As it pulled away, an almost palpable breath of relief rose into the air above the *B crew*. Jorge stood next to Justo. "What do you make of that?" he asked. "Dunno," Justo replied, "but I'm gonna find out." Jorge pondered a moment, saying "I wonder what Domingo is doing today. I know he was working on something, but he wouldn't say what it was. That's just like Domingo. He did mention something about a list and some numbers that didn't make sense. What numbers, I have no clue, but you know Domingo is good with numbers."

The lights were dimmed at 10020 Crestline Road, the headquarters for J & E Construction Company. Eddie Sorrel, Johnson, smiling Jimmy, and assorted others had gathered in one of the first floor meeting rooms, near the door. The room was unlit except for the night light in the doorway, and the forward half of the room was bathed in darkness. The group's occasional banter had flared up again but was immediately quenched by the clicking sound of a latch opening in the darkness, coming from the direction of a table at the front of the room, upon which a podium had been perched. Next to the shadow of the podium, another shadow moved suddenly, then elongated and finally moved towards the group that had assembled. Unnoticed till now, Mr. B waved a wad of money taken from his briefcase, as his tall figure and face emerged from the darkness.

The room was as quiet as a pin drop cliché until the silence was broken by the voice of *Mr B* when he spoke. "Any of you know *why* Peter hasn't picked up his bonus?" Mr. B shook the wad of bills.

After a long pause, Johnson spoke up. "*Mr B*, sir, I understood that Peter was to lay low for a while. Maybe that's what he's doing." Mr. B shook his head, "And not take with him his happy hooker money?! No. Something is wrong here. He's a better professional than to leave the car in that place, half covered. His clean up was ridiculous. None of the bodies from his previous jobs have *ever* been found, because Peter's a professional. This little pip-squeak is alive, damn it! I want him. I don't care what you have to do. Find him and make damned sure he doesn't get a chance to say any more of the prayers in his little book! Got it?" Mr. B's face had turned from the disingenuous smile that was his normal countenance, to what, Johnson was certain, was a Jackal's snarl.

Drug Dogs

Back at the apartment, Jorge and Justo sat across from each other at the table. "I can't help thinking that the police thing was all about Domingo, or maybe Peter." Justo thought for a moment, then shrugged. "Be happy, don't worry. Hey, Bobby McFerrin wrote a smart man's song, in my opinion." Jorge grinned, "What? Burying your head in the sand is smart?" "Maybe not, but ... well, over-worrying is dumb. Maybe Peter and Domingo have something going on." The spray of coffee from Jorge's mouth covered half the table.

"I'm really pissed that you made me laugh," shouted Jorge after he wiped half of his face with a sleeve, in order to soak the coffee. When Domingo hears this he's gonna keep you out of his next mealtime prayer. There'll be no sav'in for you, heathen bastard!"

Justo wiped his grin. "Does the good Lord have a sense of humor?"

"Not about that. You're going to hell Justo."

"Already am. Yeah, I'm ashamed of that. You know, my momma raised me Catholic just like you. You *are* Catholic coming straight from your mama, am I right Jorge?"

"Yes I am, or was, or something. It has been a long time since I've been to church. I still remember it though, and sometimes it makes me smile. My mother was a wonderful woman. She was the best."

"Was?"

"Yeah, that's another long story all by itself Justo. Drug dog muthas took her. When I think about what I'd like to do to them, I know I make my momma sad – up there looking down on me. She'd know I wouldn't go to heaven."

The Six Hundred

Hermosa opened the folder, and pulled the contents out of it. As she handed the pages to her companion, he asked "how many are there?" Hermosa said, "I think there are around six hundred, going back ten years." The rest are in the archive. I can't get to it." Her companion's face was grim. "Hermosa, we are going to do for these people, and we're the only ones who can." The back of the church was empty, excepting for the two slender figures. The distance closed between the two of them. A quick hug was exchanged between them, and then they were gone.

Miguel woke from his slumber. Valerie's keys were noisy in the lock. As she entered, she noticed his groggy appearance. "My sleepyhead," she said, adding "I've brought some things that will make it worth your while to get up off of that sofa!" Curious, Miguel sauntered into the kitchen where Valerie was just putting the last of the refrigerator items away. Miguel noticed the Styrofoam containers on the counter, and exclaimed "Thank you, thank you, thank you," swinging around the side of it to give Valerie a hug. His favorite Mexican food was in them, he knew. It was not the stuff that he could get in any one of the slew of Tex-Mex places close-by to the apartment. This was from the authentic restaurant that was his favorite, and quite a distance away – on the other side of town. He smiled to himself, feeling that kind of feeling one gets when someone has gone the extra mile, to do something nice for them.

They sat at the table, with Valerie munching on the rabbit food that she usually ate and that worried Miguel. You need to eat more than just that Valerie. "Tut tut," I get what I need Miguel. Just as he finished, Miguel leaned back in his chair. "Valerie. There's been some weird stuff going on again at the office. Jeff is one of the other engineers – you know, you've met him. Anyway, he was in my cubicle today complaining about his project being yanked out from under him." "Just like me, Valerie. Before it was done, they just yanked it out from under him. No explanations, nothing. It's strange as hell. I mean, if they don't trust us to do this stuff right, then why did they hire us?" Valerie's smile had gone. "I'm sure it's nothing," she said. "There's an explanation that makes sense."

"Maybe, but I'm really getting some strange vibes about things around there. Peterson comes around to my cubicle sometimes, and he just stands there, staring at my back. I can feel him staring at me, for no reason at all. The guy gives me the creeps." Valerie's smile hadn't returned, but she said "Maybe because he's responsible for all of the contracts out to ASICS Corp, he just likes to keep tabs." Miguel tipped his head back, and he started to open his mouth but stopped. He shook his head. "Valerie, I know I've never given the name of the company to you, I've never mentioned it." Miguel looked confused. Then he continued, "As part of the confidentiality agreement, we were warned never to mention any of the contract companies to anyone. Not wives, not lovers, not anybody. How did you know Valerie?" Valerie was stunned. "Buu...t maybe you dropped it by accident. You just don't remember Miguel." "No Valerie. It's a point that they underscored in a big way. A really big way. We were considered terminated for doing it. It has to do with the money that's on these patented formulas, and they want it all kept absolutely on the down-low."

"How did you know Valerie?" Miguel's face had a long hang of worry on it now, and the look he saw on Valerie's face made it worse." She reddened, and stood up, shaking her head. "You're making a big deal out of this Miguel, I'm sure you just let it slip." Now Miguel was on his feet, and he came around to where she stood. He held her waist firmly, "I need to know Valerie. Your expression said something to me a little bit ago ... God knows what, it scared the hell out of me, but you're not leveling with me. At least I get the feeling you aren't. What is going on?" Valerie fell back down into her chair. She put her head on the table and began sobbing. "It was nothing, really Miguel. It was just a little insurance ... you know, for exactly the reasons you just mentioned. I swear, I didn't want to have a secret with you, but it was already done Miguel!"

She began heaving uncontrollably, "I love you Miguel! This arrangement was not supposed to be a big deal, it was just a little keeping tabs. Please understand."

Miguel stood back. Slowly, he walked around to the other side of the table and sat down. "You were a mole from the beginning then." Valerie's face was scrunched up in a mix of fear and tears. She shook her head again. It's not anything to do with us Miguel. I love you – that's all that matters Miguel!"

Miguel sat there watching Valerie for minutes, saying nothing. Her eyes were overflowing wells of tears, begging him to forgive her. Finally, he spoke. "Valerie, please stop crying. I think we have a problem that demands we put everything else aside for awhile. I've had a feeling about my bosses and the company for a long while now. There have been other incidents ... things that happened and that I didn't relay to you because they seemed to be products of my built-in paranoia – something I developed, as a kid and later, while living in Mexico. Some things were related to the kinds of processes we were building, and the claims they were making for them – which didn't make sense. I think I just put it off, because I thought it would be different here in the states. Tell me about your handler. What does he look like?" Valerie wiped the tears from her eyes, but the pleading remained in them. After Valerie's description, Miguel sighed. "I think your handler's name is Peterson. Fits pretty well. Valerie, these people wouldn't do this as part of some kind of intellectual property protection scheme. The rationales are an order of magnitude apart, as us CEs like to say. These people are dirty. They are all dirty, really big time dirty. It's not intellectual property they are masking. It's criminality. Where did you get your cell phone Valerie?"

Valerie's features turned more guilty than she was already –

and she assumed the look of someone just made to look like a fool. "Them." Miguel stood. "Give it to me." Miguel took the phone from her hand and walked over to the corner of the kitchen, where the microwave was perched on the edge of the counter-top. Miguel pulled the battery from the phone, and held the device under the tap in the kitchen sink. Filling its interior with water, he turned, opened the microwave and tossed it it. He pressed the button. After a few minutes, the sizzling and crackling sounds stopped. He took a hot pad from the stove-top, removed the phone, and tossed it onto the floor. He smashed it with his foot until its busted pieces were spread all over the floor.

Miguel moved close to Valerie, and lowered his voice. "It's almost a certainty that this place is bugged, Valerie. They wouldn't rely on you for this. We need to find another place. Pack whatever you can get into that luggage bag I gave you, and I'll do the same. We won't be back here for awhile Valerie. I think our lives may be in danger ...

5

Wine, Women

M iguel opened the door for Valerie, and walked around to the other side of the car. He got in, turned the key, and pulled out of the space. Just above her breath, Valerie said "Thank you." "I'm trying to understand your situation, Valerie. You said you hadn't given them any more information since we – well, you know. I love you Valerie, but I'm trying to understand it all. Maybe you made some poor choices before meeting me."

"One thing *I know*, and that is this car has a tracker. There is no doubt we will be tailed. With a tracker it will be easy for them to stay back, undetected. They'll find us alone somewhere, and then ... well, let's not allow that to happen." Miguel dropped his voice to a whisper. "We're going to meet a stranger who wants to help us." Now it was Valerie's turn to look confused. Miguel continued, "A few days ago, I got a call from someone claiming that I was being tailed by people, and that it was about my work, and that I should contact her as soon as I could. At first I blew it off as ... you know ... a little ridiculous, but I've changed my mind. She gave me a number to call, and I called it while you were packing." Valerie interjected "So, now these people have the number and the details?" "I don't know. I used a phone that I keep for for a spare. It's one of those ten dollar cheapies that you're supposed to throw into your glovebox for emergencies. I bought it before Kesos gave me the company phone, and my other cell phone was kinda unreliable. Anyway, they probably know it now. I imagine we will be observed. The caller told me to take a lunch at a fast food place down the boulevard – and in fact, here it is ..." Miguel pulled into the parking lot of the place and killed the engine. After the two of them were clear of the car, Miguel said, "She'll come in and sit two tables away from us. She will have a bright blue shawl – like the mexican-american women like to wear."

About fifteen minutes passed, and the woman appeared. As promised, she wore the shawl. She bought a drink at the counter and sat down at a two seater table, two tables away from Valerie and Miguel. She drank it, and got up to leave. As she left she passed the table where Miguel sat, and dropped a wadded little piece of paper behind him. He could just see it happen out of the corner of his eye. Then, she walked out of the door.

Miguel reached down and behind himself, discretely, and picked it up. He untwisted the wrinkled note, and glanced at it. Miguel got partially out of his seat, leaned ahead, and whispered to Valerie, "Let's go." They walked out to the car, opened the doors, and got in. Miguel put the Volvo in reverse and started backing out. "What's going on?" asked Valerie. "Dunno," came back under Miguel's breath. He pulled around the back of the restaurant where the drive-through order stand was situated. There was only a little room there – just enough for a single car and no more. Just outside of the lane on the end of the lot was a dumpster, and behind it a concrete wall. Miguel pulled up to the order stand microphone. "Good afternoon" blared through the speaker. How may I help you?"

Just then Miguel heard the screeching of brakes – the familiar sound that every school kid knows well. The old church activity bus had completely blocked the lane in front Miguel's car, and at the same time a large truck pulled up behind them. Suddenly the blue shawl woman appeared at the window on Valerie's side of the car. The woman pointed at the open door on the bus. Miguel and Valerie sprinted for that door, hunching over as they went. The woman in the shawl crawled into Valerie's seat, and a companion slipped into Miguel's. The whole thing took only seconds. The Mexican American now in Miguel's car looked surprisingly like Miguel. The woman, without her shawl, did have a remarkable resemblance to Valerie. Probably, the wig had some impact on the slight of hand as it played out. The bus pulled around to the truck and bus parking area – just beyond the drive-through lane as it curved around the back of the building. The bus stopped, and a number of mexican children disembarked, walking single file with their church lady helpers into the restaurant. Miguel's car sped off and back down onto the boulevard.

The Farm

Miguel and Valerie walked into the low lying building. By morning light they found themselves out in the country, on what looked like a farm. Their tour guide said very little outside of "Follow me." Finally inside the building, he opened, "I apologize for the rough treatment on the bus – I had to get you down onto the floor in a hurry. I hope you understand."

"This is very interesting" is about all that Miguel could muster, and his lady had even less to say.

"By the way, your stuff may eventually be returned to you. We need to be careful that your luggage doesn't get followed. These people are hard to lose." A heavy set woman walked into the side door of the room. She carried a basket. "Sandwiches!" she announced. "Help yourself." Miguel and

Valerie needed no encouragement, and made use of the nice lady's offer. As they were eating their food, another form appeared in the doorway. It appeared to be a very slender man, who walked up to a chair near the couple and sat down. A tattered prayer book could be seen protruding from his rear pocket.

Thursday

Jorge and Justo sat alone in the apartment. One glance each way was enough to confirm what the other was about to say. "Something bad has happened to Domingo and Peter," finally left the lips of Jorge. "No doubt. I asked Johnson what the police cruiser was all about on Monday. He said it wasn't related to anything at the company. Wouldn't say anything else." Justo shook his head, "Did you see the pictures all over the front pages of the Anglo newspapers? Holy cow, what a fire!" Jorge nodded, "Yeah, they said the flames were visible way up on the ridge of the boulevard. Started by some mexican with an *H1-B* visa, which has already been revoked by the company he worked for. They said he had copped some trade secret patents, stole some drawings or something like that – and when they got onto him, he torched the apartment where he lived. The fire chief said the high heat probably meant an excelerant was used, and it took the whole complex down to the ground. He's a wanted man now – his picture's on the news, and he was one of our legal ones. Man, how dumb can you get?"

Justo mused, "Doesn't make sense really. Why would this Miguel guy torch his apartment. I'm sure he could get rid of any evidence more easily than that."

The men agreed that it seemed very strange. Jorge continued,

"You know, the weirdest thing about it, for me anyway, is the company they said the Miguel guy worked for. I swear I heard Johnson mention it a time or two. It was a a weird sort of name, so I remembered it."

"Well, it's time to hit the road Justo, it looks like we've got barely enough time to make it to the hell-hole gate to punch our tickets. I know neither one of us can wait to see Jimmy's big smiling teeth again ...

Tortilla Sweepings

After work Jorge had gone to his favorite unwinding place, a dive even by an illegal immigrant's standards, and a place where the tortilla chips made a crunch when Jorge walked to and from the bar to retrieve the glasses, filled with the kind of mexican spirits that brought him home. The more he drank, the more at home he felt. This particular night, he drank a lot.

By one thirty there was the last call for alcohol - and Jorge made the tortilla run one more time. When he came back to his spot, he found it had been taken. A curled over form sat in his place, some kercrotchety old fool with a whitish beard and a firm grip around an empty glass. Jorge was about to say something about the fact that there were mostly empty chairs all around, and that his half eaten sandwich wasn't for sale. He was a little bit in a mood for kicking someone's ass, although even in his sloshed-brain state he drew the line at kercrotchety old men. "Hey old man-" he began, but the kercrotchety one cut him off. "Sit down Jorge." Jorge was stunned. Instinctively he looked down at the rear pocket of the man sitting in his chair. "What the hell?" "Domingo?" "Keep it down," was the immediate response from his friend. "I'll not stay long." Jorge was too filled with questions to be calm, and the tranquilizers in his bloodstream forced them out imprudently. "Where's Peter?"

"Peter is probably still making baby faces, Jorge. There is much to say, but this is not the place or time. You are in danger Jorge. Leave the apartment – find another place – and don't go back to Jimmy's place anymore. You're not working for a construction company Jorge. Their business has not a solitary thing to do with construction. You are working for terrible men, you have no idea about the kind of evil they have in store. They're doing awful things. Just tell Justo the same thing, but not while he's in the apartment. It's bugged all to hell, and you know I don't use that word lightly. Try to remember this tomorrow Jorge. Please."

Jorge started laughing. The tranquilizers in him were turned loose, and he let out a guffaw. "Domingo, you are so damned funny." Jorge was face down on the table laughing and banging at it simultaneously.

When he looked up, Domingo was gone.

Hard Gray

The pain in his head had become intolerable. He tried to open his eyes, but couldn't do it. The light rays coming into them were as daggers into his brain. His heart raced and then, in a horrifying reversal – seemed to not pump at all. It felt like an intense pressure within him, and he couldn't release it. The pounding in his head increased, pumping up and beyond what he could stand. Finally, mercifully, the rhythm of the pain changed, and the pounding in his head became a voice, muffled and coarse and undecipherable. It repeated the same words again and again, but Justo could not understand them.

He opened his eyes once more. This time the light was less sharp. Justo became aware of the fact that he was laid out on the floor, a hard, concrete floor. His teeth grated along on it when he moved his head. He became aware that his hands were tied behind him, and that his arms ached.

His eyes tried again and again to focus, and his ears to understand the voice ...

"Justo!" Finally, Justo recognized his name. Suddenly something sharp and stinging was in his mouth and in his eyes, but cold as ice. His focus returned, and he realized that he was staring at the tip of a boot. Turning his head, he could see the bucket in the hand of the figure towering above him. Now powerful arms reached down to grab him roughly by the shirt and under his arms. Instantly, he was upright and then he wrenched backwards from the pain in his back. The strong arms shoved him forward to a spot under a light and near a small table where he was dropped unceremoniously into a chair. Wincing again, he started to fall off of the chair, but the strong arms pulled him up onto it again. "For Christ's sake Jimmy, untie his hands." Jimmy did as he was asked, "Sometimes my people get carried away with things Justo. Now, we can all be more civilized about this thing." Justo tried to steady himself on the chair by holding onto the edge of the table. Squinting, he could see the outline of Mr. B. standing next to the table, his features hidden by the bright light shining above and behind him. "All we need are a few answers Justo, and then you can go. Of course. We need to know about Domingo – you know what he's up to, don't you? Justo, we know almost everything about our people – including you – but there may be some small details that we missed. It's very important for us to know *all* the small details.   We already know all about you and your handler there at the Tortilla Palace, and of course we know that he is government.   What does that make you, Justo?"

"Dead, I imagine."

"I did say we were being civilized here, didn't I?   Come now, we needn't have anything less than an amicable conversation here. Your handler - the Fed – you know why he doesn't do this job they put you on, don't you? They don't put actual badge carriers on these jobs, don't you know Justo ... it's because you're expendable. You've been put out as shark bait – and believe me when I say it's an appropriate analogy. We don't really mess around very much Justo.   We really don't mess around at all ...

Head Ache

It had been awhile since Jorge had taken down so much tequila.   Jorge normally crawled out of bed. He was not the proverbial morning person, by any standard.   Today, Jorge crawled out of his bed, literally. He used the cheap television night stand to pull his aching body upright, and stared into the mirror hanging on the wall.   In the mirror he could see the woman – still sleeping – and who had been trolling near the exit door of the Palace when he left it.   Jorge shook his head. "Was it last night, or a week ago?" "Did I really see Domingo last night?"   Jorge wasn't sure.   He went into the bath, or what passed for one in the motel room he had taken.   He splashed water on his face and walked back into the bedroom. He sat down next to the form on the bed, jostling the woman and making her eyes open.   "Pretty eyes," he thought to himself. "What's your name? Not the one you told me last night and that I don't remember. Your real one." "Lucinda."

Jorge reached for his wallet instinctively, but it wasn't there. For a few seconds, there was a very serious locking of the eyes. Lucinda bit her lip and pulled the wallet out from inside the slipcase of her pillow. She handed it to him. "Why didn't you just take it and leave?" Jorge asked.

Now Lucinda looked a little unhappy. "I really don't know."

Jorge looked at the contents of his wallet. It was never overly full, so it was easy to count. "I imagine that the difference here is about the price for this stinky dive. Is this your regular place Lucinda?" Scrunching her eyebrows, she replied "I used your money to pay for this. Waddya think, crazy drunken man? And I'm not saying I'm regular."

Jorge smiled. Today it hurt to smile. "Ok, I need to go by something other than crazy drunken man. It's Jorge."

Shackles

Hermosa took Domingo aside. "Peter's crazy. He's in there yanking at his chain, swearing at everybody who walks in, and threatening to kill all of them." Hermosa continued, "He keeps messing with the double nuts on the muffler clamps that we put on his wrists, thinking he can rub them loose." Domingo looked concerned, "Apparently, his eyes are still foggy from the booze we gave him. I told Luis to run a spot weld on the nuts – they're not coming off. Eventually, we'll need to cut them off." Hermosa looked at Domingo, "I know you didn't like telling Luis to give him the booze. You think it's a little like using the same things as they do ... you know ... evil things."

"Truthfully, Hermosa, that booze may have a purpose under the sun. The man couldn't resist the stuff, just like he can't resist anything else in this world that suits him. The Good Lord forgives almost all the failings of man, but in Peter's case, He may have reason to pause. Peter seems to have large quantities of violence built into him, in addition to everything else. I'll pray for a conversion anyway. It's never hopeless."

Hermosa had been in there, with the booze, playing mind games with Peter ... talking the talk, but not walking it. The beast in the man associated booze and women closely, so Hermosa was able to play those age old cards in combination with her very out-of-character thespianism to separate Peter from the information she wanted. She said that she felt dirty later, and was going to see the padre at the church for it. She mused, "The government has other options. We don't. We have a half dozen very brave ninety eight pound church ladies – thank the Lord for that - and Luis, Miguel, and of course you, Domingo."

"We're just not physically fearsome. We will need all our prayers plus a little." Hermosa added, "I think Peter is angry about the shackles." Domingo interrupted, "We didn't have any choice about that either Hermosa. You know that neither Luis nor myself can be seen very well in profile, thanks to the way God made us, and I surely couldn't expect the Saturday evening Spanish mass church lady choir at St. Augs to keep him from getting loose and then getting us all killed."

Hermosa smiled, "there you do have a pretty good point." Domingo continued, "We've probably saved a couple lives already. We can't turn him over to police because they'll arrest us and not him. I don't have quite enough evidence to make the authorities stop in their tracks, and that's what it would take to make them look into something on the say-so of an illegal."

Valerie was in the farmhouse, helping with the group meal that was being prepared. "I just don't know why I can't use Domingo's cell phone," she said. Florencia looked at her, and shrugged. "I don't know much about electronic things, but both Domingo and Luis have mentioned that cell phones are very easily compromised devices that can be tracked."

Floriencia went on, "I understand that it's just a matter of calling the wrong number, even by accident, and then it's all over. That's why Domingo keeps the only cell phone. He's trying to prevent any accidents. These drug people could come down here and kill all of us easily. They'd only need to know where we are to do it ... and they want to do it ... *badly*."

"They have their people spread throughout industry and in the biggest companies. Even the telephone company could be involved, or have a lot of people on their payroll."

Tony

Tony came into the room, and Mr. B stood back. "Well, I expected this of you Justo. Just the cut of your jibe told me you were a hard case. I really didn't want to turn you back over to Tony. I'm sure you didn't appreciate his methods of persuasion the first time." Tony had been the one to beat Justo into a state of unconsciousness, and now he stood in the arch of the door, grinning a not so benevolent grin. "F---ing bastard-" was all that Justo could manage before Jimmy's hard fist nailed him to the floor like a pike of roof shingles. Jimmy jumped down on the unlucky man's back, to tightly rope his hands together again. Then he tied a loop almost as tightly around Justo's neck, and jumped up. He tossed the end of the leash to Tony, who swept it up into his hand.

"Take him out to the usual place" was the last thing Justo heard from Mr. B.

6

Lucinda

Jorge sat across from Lucinda in the booth at Ed's Taco Villa. "I can't believe I'm eating this stuff," he said. "My momma's probably worrying about me now."

Lucinda snickered, "I don't think it's the tacos she's worried about!"

"You sure do joke a lot about *your profession*" retorted Jorge. "Never said it was *my profession*." Jorge gave her a look of disbelief. Lucinda scrunched her eyes.

"Lucinda, you got me for part of what you would have gotten me for anyways. First I buy your lunch, and now dinner, and I don't even remember a *thing*. Peter would be laughing at me now."

"How about if I tell you it was real good, Jorge?" Jorge thought, "Real good was the head-banger I put on last night. Seriously, it was unhealthy, even by my standards. I'm trying to remember what Domingo said to me last night. It was close to *lights out* time for me, but I swear he was going on-and-on about my company being out to get me – you know – *maybe even to kill me,* or something like that. I seem to remember that he said I shouldn't go back to the apartment because they'd be waiting for me. Crazy stuff."

Lucinda was giving him a little bit of a come-on smile. "I'm too hung over Lucinda, and now, thanks to you, I'm broke. You need to save that for *The Palace* parking lot." Lucinda's smile erased, and she actually looked a little insulted. "I'm thinking I might not hang out around there anymore, Jorge." Jorge tilted his head back, giving Lucinda the *please get serious* look, and followed that with "I should take you to wherever you stay now, Lucinda." Lucinda looked at him and shook her head slowly. "Nah. I think I'll just stay with you for awhile, you know, and hang out. You like me."

Jorge's eyes widened. "Oh my ga-" Lucinda interrupted "Let's not swear. Your momma's already worried, remember? She's worried that you won't join up with her someday." Jorge became serious. "How did you know about my mother?"

"Two things Jorge, since you maybe aren't a student of people. First, the look in your eyes when you said it. Secondly, you used words that implied that she could see you now. Pretty simple, huh?"

"What are you, a psych major? They hang around at the Palace now?" "Yeah, my own mother said I was the smarty - that I'd do something to get myself out of the grotto. Boy was she ever wrong."

"Where is your mother now, Lucinda?" "Jorge - she's in the same place as yours."

Pleasant Bend

Hermosa brought the tray into the coop where Peter was restrained. He watched her as she put the tray down on the wooden floor - the floor that was stained from the booze and all of the food that Peter had tossed in fits of anger. Hermosa picked up the broom handle that was leaning in the corner. Carefully, she touched the broom handle to the edge of the tray and pushed it towards Peter. "Shucks, church lady, you really do have an irritating sort of standoffish attitude, especially since it's already our third date."

"You can do something other than curse and growl. I'll make a note of it."

"I bet I did more than curse and growl the other night, damn-it. Church ladies aren't supposed to be that wicked. They're going to kick you out of the cloister."

Hermosa looked a little confused. "For Satan's right hand beast you do have some good grammatical habits. I'll make a note."

"I went to college lady. Of course, it was paid for by my body and not my brains. I used my body to get through school. I have a good one – almost as good as yours, church lady." The church lady was embarrassed. "It was only for the greater good – and I've already seen a priest about it."

"I bet you have." Hermosa turned and walked towards the door. As she touched the latch to open it, she turned around. "Maybe I can bring him back for an exorcism."

It was almost exactly twenty five miles from the farm to the midtown bridge, but it was only six miles to Pleasant Bend – a spot on the road that would barely deserve a little map dot, even if it were on one. Its claim to fame was its only industry, an old sugar beet processing plant. The plant was the reason for the town's nickname: stinky town. For the wayfarer who could stand the late summertime stench, stinky town offered a beer and *carry out* supplies store, along with a small grocery. This was the place for resupply of the farm's storage sheds and pantry. It was a place where one could be seen by a very predictable and small group of people. It was perhaps a place where a little group of church ladies and their diminutive male counter contingent could lay low and mostly out of sight.

The grocery was decidedly old time vintage – with wooden plank floors and the open rafter ceiling that told of days before agriculture department inspections. On this day, Florencia and Valerie stood in one of the only two isles in the place, hashing over what to buy and how much of it.

Florencia excused herself to use the ladies room. The moment the door closed behind her farm-mate, Valerie was out of the front door and around to the side of it. As she stood near the ice-cube self-serve chest, she pulled the little plastic device out of her purse. In a moment, she had dialed the memorized number on Domingo's cell phone.

As Florencia returned to the section of the store where she had been, Valerie was standing exactly where Florencia left her, still studying the same bag of flour. As Valerie looked up, she said, "The bleached flour smells better than what's in the bin. I think we should go with it, even if it's a little more expensive." Florencia agreed, and the two of them carried their baskets – each heaping full – to the single counter in the little store. The young woman at the counter checked them out. Valerie read the name tag on the young woman's chest. "Melissa," she read out loud, "I bet you are Melissa Elderman, just like the name on the sign over the door - "Elderman's Grocery." Melissa responded with a bright smile. "Good guess."

Valerie continued, "I'm surprised you don't have one of those old time cash registers, to go with the patina and character of your nice little store." Melissa smiled again, saying "We do!" as she pointed to the old, well worn and black painted register, now partially covered with a sheet of meat-wrapping paper on the rear portion of the counter. "My parents talked Grandpa into this new one with all the bells and whistles. They said it made his work easier with the way it sends reports back to the computer in the office." Melissa pointed to the half opened door and the unlighted space behind it.

"Grandpa really complained a lot about the new register while he was getting used to it, but he's great with it now. I can't keep up with him. The other day, he was playing some kind of game on the office computer. I had to scold him of course. He thought I was being pretty funny - scolding my Grandpa for goofing off."

"So ... mom and pop are not around today?" "Really, I work for my Grandpa - and he's running an errand." The two women thanked Melissa for bagging the groceries, and they walked out to the truck. Valerie inquired of Florencia, knowing that she had lived for a while in the area. "Does it really stink so badly when sugar beet time comes around? I mean, does the town deserve the name?" "You have no idea Valerie. It took me years to get used to it. Hopefully, this craziness will be done by the time the beets are ready, and you and the others will all be safe - and probably not around here anymore. Not that I'm pushing you away, you understand." Valerie liked Florencia. She seemed old world - and her age probably synchronized pretty well with the old days and the old ways, although Valerie had some difficulty guessing the number of birthdays that had passed in her friend's life. Florencia was one of those lucky ones who ages gracefully. Valerie mused, "maybe all of the fresh farm food was part of Florencia's secret." The others had commented that Florencia's voice was still the best in the Spanish mass choir, another thing which seemed out of character for a woman not so young any more. Florencia seemed very wise in some way.

Florencia turned the wheel of the truck to make the turn into the driveway at the farm, and drove back to a mud-buried stone and weed sprinkled area. The single width parking space was just off to the left of the coop where Peter was restrained. As the two of them exited the truck with the groceries, with one bag in each woman's hands, Hermosa opened the door of the coop and stepped out. She had the tray in her hands, and she waved at the newly arrived friends-with-food.

Hermosa was smiling, then grinning, and Florencia's baffled look prompted a response from the woman. Hermosa shook her head, "Oh it's nothing ... silly jokes ... the rotten little son of Satan can be funny sometimes, I'll admit. At least it's better than threatening to break my neck." The newcomers exchanged glances, but there was no grin or smile in either of them. "Hermosa, you know- " "I'm not crazy!" Hermosa shot back. "It's just that he occasionally comes through as human. I imagine that this is true of the most evil of people. You needn't worry about me."

1032 Whistleview

Jorge and Lucinda disembarked from the bus, down only a couple blocks from the apartment at number 1032. They left the old beat-up company truck, the one that should have been their transportation, at the Palace. It was one of those vehicles that had become finicky in its old age, requiring an exact sequence of events, a precise number of accelerator pumps and a certain timing on the starting routine before it would run. Jorge had been too drunk to get it right, and Lucinda ran the battery down trying to start the cantankerous old thing. She had walked, and he had stumbled to the forty-winks, located in a convenient place relative to the Palace.

When Jorge and Lucinda returned to give it another try, it refused to work, even with a passer-by's good will and the use of his jumper cables. So, Jorge decided to let the company deal with the truck, and the couple grabbed a bus.

As they approached the building, Jorge noticed that Justo's car was gone, and that there was another one parked in the place that Justo normally used. Jorge began, "I wonder where Justo is today." He was about to say something more, but the motion of the door opening at 1032 caught his eye and first syllable before he could breath it into the air. Justo grabbed Lucinda by the arm, and pulled her back. "That's Johnson and "toothpaste commercial" Jimmy coming out of my apartment, Lucinda. Wonder what's up with that." Just then Johnson turned to look in the direction of the couple. In a heartbeat, Johnson slapped Jimmy on the shoulder and pointed. Instantly, both men started running hard in Jorge's direction. Jorge jumped, "What in the-?- Lucinda - they're looking unfriendly – and I think I see a holster under Jimmy's coat." Simultaneously pulling Lucinda's arm and turning in the opposite direction, Jorge shouted "Run!"

Lucinda needed no more encouragement – and soon was flying alongside Jorge and then was out in front of him.

Lucinda outpaced Jorge, as the booze toxins in his legs held him back. Jimmy was hard on Jorge's heels, and the two of them ran headlong into the short leg of a gully that wound around a little bump of a hill. The gully didn't go all the way around the circumference of the mound of earth, and instead it was stopped up by a concrete wall, formed into a U shape that served as the dug out and the pad for a rust and green colored dumpster.

Jorge stopped short at the wall. He saw a chink of concrete

that made a toehold about four feet up the wall and he put his foot into it. Shoving off of the dumpster, he purchased a grip on the top of the wall and started to heave himself upward. His upward progress was painful, as the toxins were in his arms as well as his legs. As his body tugged against the shortest leverage of his ascent, as his arms were folded back on themselves, his face was smashed up against the concrete wall.

Jimmy had grabbed onto Jorge's left leg, and in a violent motion, he yanked it away from the crevice in the wall. The two of them fell into a heap on the cold concrete of the floor under the dumpster. Jimmy broke loose of Jorge, and jumped up. In a second, his nine millimeter weapon was pointed at Jorge's head.

Jorge turned to look in the direction of the sound of the white SUV as it came to rest just short of the dumpster. Johnson climbed out of the truck, and walked back to where Jorge had been sequestered by the wad-cutter bullet at the back of the blue steel barrel being pointed at him. As usual, the gun holder was smiling, showing Jorge his big Bright-White commercial teeth. "We should just pop him here," came from the walking toothpaste advertisement, and then "He'll be no more useful than Justo." Jorge's eyes lit up, "You have Justo?" The captors just looked at each other, nodding their heads and snorting. "As a matter of speaking" finally left Johnson's lips. Johnson walked around to where Jorge was now standing, and then moved to his backside. He told Jorge to put his hands behind his back. "Go to hell," Jorge said in response, and then "I have no idea why you are doing this. What is going on? You're both crazy."

The smiling man stretched out his arm and moved the gun up, carefully aligning it on the space between Jorge's eyes. "You need to do as the boss man says Jorge, or we'll change our plans and leave a little surprise for the dumpster service truck driver. We wouldn't want to do that. He might be squeamish." Jorge gave Jimmy an unpleasant look, but he complied, and Johnson put a double loop plastic cable wrap around Jorge's wrist. When they were secure, he pushed Jorge forward roughly, and pointed to the back of the SUV, saying "We need to take a little ride, Jorge."

The ride seemed to go on for a long time, and Jorge's face down position on the floor of the SUV, one that caused his head to bang continually into the carpet on every bump, didn't make it any more pleasant. At some point, perhaps thirty minutes elapsed time - in Jorge's estimation, the SUV swerved onto a side road. The sound of the SUV's tires on the gravel road beneath the floor of the truck told Jorge that the destination was close by. It seemed that there was a grade, and the engine snarled a little bit as Johnson gunned it. A few times, the tires let loose with a spit of stones. Then the feeling was of going downhill, and the SUV picked up speed for another thirty seconds, then slowed and swerved hard to the left. Jorge's head bounced hard against the door panel, reigniting the headache that he had nearly conquered.

The SUV stopped.

The three of them got out, walked over to the side of the stone lane, and drained their weeds. Jorge had to pop the fake handcuffs off of his wrist in order to drain his. He might have done it with them on, but he would have gotten his pants wet. Johnson pulled a coupla brewskies out of the cooler, and passed em' out. A good time was had by all. "We really had those silly-ass readers fooled," said Jorge. Jimmy nodded, "Let's high five that one!"

The whole crew had gathered in the short building. That's what they called the largish, but low lying building that served as the main meeting place for members of the *farm*. Miguel was there, as well as Luis, Hermosa, Florencia, and the others. Domingo was sitting on the table at the side of the building, tapping his feet on the old wooden chair that now served as his footstool. Now he began, "This is going to be dangerous for Luis, but he's the only one they won't recognize. We will need to pray for him. If he doesn't make contact with us after three days, we will know the probable result." Luis nodded slowly. He had taken the job without question, knowing already the likely result of failure. Not as religious a man as Domingo, he had benefited from the man's charisma, and had become spiritually imbued with some of the leader's energy and spark. He needed no additional base level motivation, however; as his brother's name was on the list of six hundred. Often, as the group organized their daily activities, he could be heard repeating the words of Domingo, "We will do for these people."

Alejandro would be the contact point for Luis. He was not an official farm member – and did not stay there – but he was a trusted one. Domingo was certain of this man's thoughts and loyalties, and the two had forged a friendship via the weekly assemblies at St. Augs. Alejandro would isolate the group, and make it just one step more difficult to poison the only defense they really had: anonymity. Alejandro was putting himself in serious harm's way – but not so much as Luis.

Miguel asked, "Does anyone know where Valerie is? I haven't seen her yet this morning." Domingo shrugged, "Haven't seen her, has anyone else?" Florencia piped up, "I saw her leaving in the truck Domingo. You might think she'd have mentioned something about it to you or somebody else." Domingo added, "Well, maybe she's on an urgent mission to the grocery. She knows that her face is dangerous for all of us – so I hope to God she's doing it in stinky town." Domingo shook his head, then continued, "Do you have your new identity, Luis?" "Yes. You know, the cards look real good. Better than any I've used before. Florencia's friend is an artiste, by any standard. I've never seen better work." Domingo agreed, saying "Let's hope that our little mission goes as smoothly as the fake cards." Maria brought in the food, and the Saturday Evening St. Aug's choir girls and boys began to eat. Tipping his glass of Mexican soda, Luis quipped, "I make a toast to this being one of many wonderful meals we will have together." He paused, and then added, chuckling nervously " ... and not my last supper."

The Little Room

The little apartment was cheap, and that's about all that could be said for it. There was the quaint little kitchen tucked into a nook off of the corner of the main room, and filled with appliances that looked like things that didn't work anymore, and that one might find in a second hand store on the poor side of town. There was a bath - even smaller than the kitchen, and cut into the opposite corner of the room.

The main room was spartan, although it contained an eclectic combination of furniture pieces and parts. Those were deposited in sufficient quantity to make a convincing case for the idea that someone actually did live in the place. The fridge contained a collection of the kinds of things that you would expect to find in a woman's apartment.

The lone occupant of the room sat in one of the art deco chairs, nervously tapping her feet while watching the tip of the second hand quiver as it clicked out its little mouse sounds. The woman bolted upright at the sharply louder tapping sound coming from the direction of the door. A moment passed, and then there came a more urgent and rapidly paced knocking on the door. The woman stood up from her seat, her face a mix of anxiety and resignation. She pulled open the door. The figure of a man stood there, and atop the figure was the unchanging dour face of Peterson, standing in the arch of the entryway. "Hello Valerie."

The Interview

Luis sat in the grubby little office, along with a tassel of others – mostly younger and mostly bigger. Luis's turn came and he moved into the hot seat. In succession, the others, likewise, moved one seat closer to his. The little office was now warm and cramped, as the interview process afforded no privacy. Luis handed the little packet to the interviewer. Jimmy pulled the ID cards from the packet and laughed. "I've seen this guy's work before. He's a dandy." Luis didn't flinch, and responded in a nondescript way, one that carried a hidden piece of information, and the unsaid "Oh well, I guess I'll try one door down the street" body language. Slowly, Jimmy dropped his thin-skin stretched smile a little, and then he said in a matter of fact fashion "Notta problem here Jose. We are equal opportunity." He let out a guffaw, and tossed the cards and the packet back to Luis. "I wouldn't suggest using those fakes any place else Jose, my boy. You caught me in a good mood, and I'm needing masonry guys. You're on, you lucky ambre. See that little door over there. Go over there and get set up with a schedule. R.M. will take caraya. Ok?" Jimmy pushed away from the desk, and swung his chair around in an arc that put his back to most of the interviewees. Seeming not to care about the others in line, he did a not so great job of concealing himself as he took a line of cocaine. Throwing his head back, he spun the chair back around, stopping it when it was square with the hot seat. "Next!"

Two weeks later ...

Domingo was sitting in the last row of pews when Alejandro plopped down beside him, startling him and making him jump. The "Yeow!" was followed by a firm handshake and a grip on Alejandro's shoulder. "Tell me all, Alejandro." Shaking his head, the younger man started out, "Luis has taken down the license plate numbers on most of the vehicles coming and going from the company – and especially the trucks. He tried to get DOT numbers when he could." He said some of the trucks were not marked with any other identifiers. He looked for your other friends from crew B – you know, Pedro, Roddy, Little Jorge, and all of the others. They're gone Domingo! All of them! Twelve guys! He asked around with the new guys on the crew, but none of them had any idea what happened to the crew you worked with. He said he's tried to get into the office when he could be alone – but it's been tough going. So far, no dice on that score."

Domingo thanked Alejandro, and the two men exchanged firm shoulder shakes. Domingo got up to leave, and said, "Give me a few minutes, and then use that other door to leave." Alejandro nodded, and Domingo was gone.

It would be a couple days before Rosa could track the numbers through her friend at the DMV. It was then a couple more days before Rosa's other friend could get the fire schematics. Rosa had convenient friends. Rosa was a gabber. She talked constantly, and always seemed to know something about any topic brought up in conversation by the people she met. Additionally, she had a magnificent command of the English language. Most of the people she met had not even a suspicion that she was an illegal immigrant.

It was evening before Rosa brought the schematics into the short building where Domingo and Miguel were sitting. Miguel was good with schematics and blueprints. It didn't matter if the drawings were for chemical plants or for anything else. His normal work revolved around lot's of mechanical issues related to the building of chemical processing facilities. He pointed at a section of the blueprint that Domingo had flattened out onto the largest table.   At the top of the large unfolded sheet were the words *Fire Department Diagram for ASICS Corporation, Buildings A and B, 6322 Departure Drive.*

"This is where we gain entry Domingo."   Domingo could see the hollow look on Miguel's face.

"I'm sorry, Miguel ... about Valerie."   Miguel tilted his head, looking up at the dirty old rafters hanging above him. The side of his mouth twisted into a frown. "I just don't understand what's happened. If she had double crossed us, we'd be dead already. Yet, I can't believe I misjudged her feelings that badly. I'm a total moron when it comes to women, I recognize that as a fact, but I'm still just so damned sure that I know how it is with us." And then – "They may have gotten her. That's in line with the truck being found by the county sheriff, south of stinky town - in that little town of North Creek." Miguel's look turn down to desperate.   "Or ..." Miguel couldn't finish his sentence.   Domingo put his hand on Miguel's shoulder. "I don't think so Miguel. I'm pretty good at hunches, and I don't think so."

7

Like Rats

T he deputy stood next to the old woman, who pushed a grayish black, stringy strand of hair from her eyes. "Well, she was a week late on her rent, so I came over to see what was the matter. Then – well, you understand, I don't just open up the apartment whenever I like – but I did peek into the window when she didn't answer my knock. I saw the broken lamp on the floor, and the chair tipped over." The woman glanced at the broken piece of furniture, still lying where it fell. "I thought it looked suspicious, and so I let myself in. It was then that I noticed the blood on the table – which you can see right there." The old woman pointed at the spot. It was not very big, but had to come from a pretty serious nosebleed in any case. The deputy spoke next. "Well, I ran an inquiry, using the information that you gave me on the telephone, and the report came back negative. Really – it came back worse than negative. We couldn't find anyone with that license number in the system. We didn't even find a Valerie Star."

The deputy let a noisy breath of air rush through his nose, "We have a lot of people running under the radar these days, and especially the immigrants, of course. Was this Valerie lady Hispanic?" The old woman shook her head. "Not by my estimation." The deputy continued, "It could be someone hiding from an abusive spouse, or a variety of other things. Really, with the bogus ID we have very little to go on.   We don't even have a picture to post. Just let us know if she comes back, so we can put some kind of final notation in the blotter."

Departure

Miguel pushed the limb aside so that Domingo could get through. The two of them squatted next to the row of shrubbery lining the road in front of building A. Miguel breathed, "Stare at any spot just above the cement fence, maybe a foot above it for a while. Tell me what you see." Domingo looked at his friend with an expression of total non-comprehension, but he complied. Twenty seconds passed, and he said "There's just a faint line of light. You can barely see it even though it's pretty dark out here." "Yup", came back from Miguel. "It's near infrared laser. And it's less detectable than regular IR security beams." Domingo was the thinner of the two men, so he went first.

The grating over the sewer came away easily, but it made a clanging sound as Domingo butterfingered it, letting it fall into the concrete gully below the outlet. Wasting no time, Domingo tested the hole. "It's so tight. It's awfully tight, Miguel. It's going to be slow." Domingo tied the rope around his feet, as Miguel rolled out a few feet of it. Miguel unslung the heavy backpack he had been carrying, and dropped it onto the embankment. He pulled a smaller bag out of it, and handed it to Domingo. "I hope it works. You'll have to push it ahead of you. It'll be an inch at a time. I hope we have that much time." As if in response to the words, a small van's brakes screeched, and it quickly slowed to an unexpected stop about two hundred feet away, and in the main drive leading to building A. Before the muffled sounds of two voices could be heard by Domingo and Miguel, they were already both lying face down in the dirt next to the shrub line. Moving his head to look at where they had been, Miguel's heart skipped a beat. His backpack lay just next to the concrete of the gully. Worse, the bright white rope coil lay in the gully. Surely, thought Miguel, it would be noticed if a beam of light were pointed near it. The voices grew louder as the two security guards approached the area, and now the powerful beams from their flashlights missed the rope and backpack by only a few yards. The beams flashed back and forth twice more, higher up on the embankment, and then they went out. A distinct "It was nothing." was announced by one of them, and they retreated to their vehicle.

Neither man had moved a muscle, and perhaps had not even breathed. As the van turned to reverse itself, Miguel finally inhaled, taking some of the loose soil from below the hedge up into his nose. "That was close," came as a whisper from Domingo. Domingo was again at the tiny opening of the pipe. Into it he went, and when the concrete coffin had completely encased his shoulders, his motion slowed to a jerky crawl. "Three yanks and you pull me out, right?" Miguel nodded in his nervousness, not thinking that Domingo could no longer see him. "Right?" Domingo queried more urgently. "Right."

Twenty minutes into the pipe, Miguel noticed the rope movement had stopped. Miguel nodded to himself. That was the seventy five foot point, exactly where the first animal gate would be. The blueprints were correct. In the pipe, Domingo pulled the tiny oil pressure powered, hydraulic jack from the heavy canvas sack. He noticed the rating plate on the side of it. Twelve tons, it said, and he muttered, "I pray to Jesus that it's enough." He pulled a tiny drill motor from the canvas sack, as he repositioned the flashlight on his headband. "God, I hope this noise is not too much ..." he thought out loud, as the masonry bit cut into the wet concrete and spit little stones out in front of his nose. He pushed lightly on the trigger, turning the bit slowly, and in several minutes he managed an inch and a half. Now he put the steel anchor shaft into the hole, and attached the jack base to it. He attached the short piece with the Y groove to the animal gate. The space was confining to the point where every move required both a conscious effort and a little pain, but he worked the short handle of the hydraulic cylinder. Five minutes passed and the gate bowed outward. The barrier kept giving in to the pressure, bending instead of breaking. The metal, in Domingo's estimation, was not as thick as Miguel had guessed. Domingo decided to put another hole into the concrete, positioning it closer to the gate, but he gave the jack handle one last push. The crusted gate broke loose with the cracking sound of brittle, rusted metal.

Domingo remembered Miguel saying that there would be one more gate, near the end of the pipe, an additional one hundred and twenty feet ahead. Outside, Miguel had arranged the rope to run linearly along the edge of the gully, in case the security corps came along again. He sat there in the dark, feeding the rope in, measuring it as it went.

Suddenly, the movement of the rope stopped again. The rope measure was still far short of the next gate. Miguel waited anxiously, peering into the hole after his friend.

Domingo clasped his hands tightly over his nose. Now, his eyes watered. A minute passed, and he had to let in a breath. The vapor stung at his nose, and then became a burning sensation within his lungs. The water sloshed down around him, drenching the top portion of his clothing that had until now remained dry. The overpowering chemical stench of bleach mixed with something else overtook him, and he lay unconscious in the concrete coffin. At the opening Miguel could now smell the noxious odor. The effluent came gurgling and bubbling down into the gully. Watching it, he knew it may have overcome Domingo. Miguel tugged on the rope, hoping to get a tug back. There was nothing. A minute later, he tugged again, but still there came no answering tug. Nothing. Miguel stared at the limp rope.

Domingo became aware that his head lay on the wet concrete, and that his hair was sopped. The flashlight on his headband beamed into the side of the pipe, and he stared at the little bright spot for a minute. His throat was dry, but he slowly became conscious of the fact that he was breathing ... and that he was alive. He gathered up his tools, and put them into the wet canvas bag. Miguel let out a sigh of relief as the rope inched forward again.

As Domingo closed in on the final gate, he could see the light from the room with the floor grate. It was a grayish light, but Domingo welcomed it. The animal gate was, perhaps, only twenty feet back from the grate, and Domingo had to be very careful about the noise of the drill. He listened intently for any indication of people near the exit of his tomb, and then let the bit of the drill turn slowly for a short while. He repeated the process, again and again, until the little anchor slid home to the mark on its side. This gate gave way easily, as the chemical agents had prematurely aged the old iron. He shoved the crusty piece of metal aside. Arching his back slightly to avoid the sharp ends of the gate, he moved past it. As he reach the floor grate, he saw that it too, would require the jack. Luckily, the final barrier did not require the drill. There was a convenient ledge onto which the little hydraulic tool could be balanced while it would do its magic one more time. Domingo again listened intently for sounds of humans. Hearing nothing for a long while, he pushed slowly upwards on the grate. Its mooring had been pulled loose of the concrete anchors, and it floated in its beveled slot. Slowly, he pushed it aside, and when it was clear, he hoisted himself up onto the floor of the room. Five tugs was the signal that Domingo had met with success. Now, Miguel would attach the rope to himself, and enter the pipe. This trip for Miguel would be more quickly done than Domingo's, because Domingo could help by pulling the second man through the narrow pipe. As Miguel slid along in the pipe, he was helped greatly by the tough plastic roll out sled – one of a type sold to the parents of kids for their winter fun.

Miguel had carefully marked the rope with paint on the spots that coincided with the animal gates, so that Domingo would know to stop pulling. Thusly, Miguel could navigate the sharp edges of the broken gates as he passed them. Soon, both men stood in the gray lit room. Both were drenched with God-knows-what from head to foot. Miguel was bleeding from a few brushes between the concrete and his knuckles. His shirt was torn on the left shoulder, and there was some blood from the abrasions there. Domingo was cut on his hands, from working with the sharp metal. Otherwise, both men seemed to be OK, as they took inventory of themselves and each other.

Miguel tapped Domingo's shoulder, "Look there!" The hole that had been their unwelcome confinement had two other pipes leading into it. Both of them were of a smaller diameter, perhaps half the size of the main pipe that had been their entry point. One of the pipes looked dry, but from the other came the ooze of a brownish black substance, and masses of it hung down from the end of the pipe like dripping dark icicles. "Strange looking stuff Domingo. What the hell is it?" "Dunno."

The room they found themselves standing in appeared to be a

garage, and now they could see that half of the hole was shadowed by the five ton truck parked above it. Domingo pushed the grate back into its beveled groove. At the end of the room there could be seen a door. Other than for the double high truck garage doors, it was the only way out of the room. Miguel looked at Domingo, who shrugged and pointed at the door. "Let's go." There was a pane of glass in the door of the type used for security purposes – a composite of metal reinforcing wires and thick clouded glass. Peering through, Miguel could see the fuzzy outline of a long corridor inside. "Probably locked" guessed Domingo. Miguel pushed on the handle, and the door swung open.

They stepped into the corridor, and walked lightly along one side of it, stopping at each opening and carefully looking into them. There seemed to be a series of large, empty rooms, walled with concrete block and having stark, cold unpainted concrete floors. They passed three such rooms when a noise halted them. The low pitch moaning sound seemed to be coming from the opposite end of the corridor, Miguel looked at Domingo. "It's what we're here for Miguel. No backing out now." Miguel nodded, and the two men continued – lightly, as before – to walk towards the sound. Another fifty feet, and it became evident that the sound they heard was not one sound, but multiple sounds, some lower and some higher pitched. Then, out of the low droning chorus came a more disturbing sound - seemingly but not certainly human. It shrieked out its wail in a long guttural scream, a cry of agony that stopped both men in mid-step. There was the sound of a door slamming shut, and two men appeared from around the corner of an adjoining corridor, walking fast in the direction of the scream. "Let's get some tranquilizer into 'em. C'mon, let's keep the noise tamped down here!" came from one of them. Neither of the newcomers saw Miguel or his partner, and the latter party slipped into an opening to the right of them.

Ten minutes later, the two men returned and went down the corridor from whence they had come. Miguel continued to walk in the direction of the scream. Domingo hesitated. Miguel gave him a smile hanging with wry gallows humor, "It's what we're here for, remember?" "Did I say that?" muttered Domingo as he followed his friend's lead.

They reached the opening to the room at the end of the corridor. There was no motion within, but the low moaning sound started up again, now coming from a small rectangular stall, about twice the size of a small shower enclosure. These structures lined the room, left to right. About as tall as a man, they were each strung with black plastic, which was draped around them, and hanging down onto the concrete floor. Domingo could see a tag affixed to each stall. The tags each had some type of identifier written on them ... "1A, 2B ... " muttered Miguel. Domingo counted the rows – four deep and eight wide.

"If someone comes, we'll just slip into one of these stalls Miguel. Our odds will be one in thirty two of being found." Miguel's mathematical mind realized the mistake, but he nodded anyway and walked in the direction of the loudest of the sounds. Now the disturbing fluid-like noises emanated from several of the other stalls.

Miguel reached the center of the room. The target was just ahead of him, on the other side of a massive central floor drain. Miguel stopped up short. His canvas shoes slipped in the muck – but no – *it was not muck*. "Christ!" he said too loudly, as Domingo flapped his hands and arms down violently in a protest of Miguel's indiscretion ...

8

Boyfriend

The police sergeant looked at the young woman. "Maria, your mother was trying to do well for you when she named you. Why don't you try to make her proud?" "That's what my boyfriend and I are gonna do – make her proud. We're gonna have a respectable family and kids and stuff. But first you gotta save him from these crazy people." The sergeant frowned. "You're worse than the illegals. You know you take way more of my time, my valuable state-paid-for time that I could and should be spending in the pursuit of the real citizens who are being raped, murdered, and/or robbed, and who have last names. Instead, you want me to go running after this Jorge guy that you met in a bar, probably banged for your regular "tip," and who has, apparently, no last name. How many times have I arrested you ... ummmm ... "Lucinda?"

Drug Dog Muthas

Jimmy pushed Jorge ahead, prompting an immediate curse word from the prisoner. "Keep it up music box. We can make this short or long. Personally, I like long." They approached the building. It was a nondescript double story brick building. Weather and time had not completely washed the painted words off of the sign hanging on the side of it. "Wes" was followed by faint markings and the letters "uarry." Shortly, the trio stood in front of a small freight door on the lane side of the building.   Jimmy keyed the lock while Johnson reached down and pulled the heavy door upwards. "Ladies first," the toothy one announced.

The air in the building was wrong. Dead wrong.   Jimmy pushed Jorge along in the semi-darkness.   Abruptly, Jimmy stopped, "This is your train station music box!"   Johnson fiddled with some keys for a moment, finally producing one, "I think this is it. The key – that is. It's not "it" for Jorge." Jimmy bristled, "Yeah – I know, they want us to keep him alive for awhile. Don't ask me why. If we put music box in the cooler, he'll suffocate. I was looking forward to dreaming about that tonight. It's your lucky day." Johnson mused, "We could run a chain through the door, so that it would be ajar by an inch. Music box may have to stand there next to the door to snatch his breath, but that's OK.   It'll give him something to do." Jimmy snickered,   "Well, I left a half dozen unprocessed in there. He'll have his nose close to the crack, believe me." Both men let out a roar of laughter, and Johnson swung the door open. "Geeeeaaawwd" came outta Johnson, "How long they been in there?"   "After three days in the truck, a coupla weeks here." Both men fell into bent over laughter again.

"Let's get the hell outta here. It's making me sick." Jimmy kicked at Jorge's lower torso and loins, sending him reeling backwards into the cool darkness.   There was a rustling of chains, and all became quiet. After a little while, there were muffled voices and a truck door slamming.

Jorge couldn't breath. It wasn't for lack of air. His lungs didn't want to take it in.   He remembered his poor old mama and the days when the power went out, which it did – sometimes for a week.   And then, sometimes, his mama couldn't pay the bill. He remembered how rank the meat was when it had to be taken out a week later. But this was much worse. This was ten times worse. The thick, sick vapor convulsed him into gag reflex, but he fought it back. He fought it back again and again ... and again, and then he wretched. On his knees he wretched. When there was nothing but clear liquid he reached the door. Oddly, the bitter of his own vomit seemed like relief for him. Slowly, he regained a rhythm of shallow breathing. He couldn't leave the door. Under no circumstances would he leave the door. He worked his fingers around the edge of it and jammed them in. Then he hung there.

The darkness was not complete, and as the hours went by, Jorge's eyes adjusted to the new condition. He had only briefly turned away from the crack in all those hours. When he had, then – involuntarily - his head had jerked back to the thin line of air and lesser darkness. His head was as that of a rider on a roller coaster at the moment it takes its plunge. A force of gravity brought him back into position. Slowly, his senses acclimatized to the vaporous stench, and now out of the corner of his left eye he could see the gray forms of the corpses. Corpses is a word that implies discrete wholes, but these were different. There didn't seem to be any one corpse, but instead a tangle of limbs that had incorrect connections to other sections of the mass. Only one corpse seemed whole. It was also the only one with clothing.

For a long time, Jorge stared at that corpse. It was familiar in the way it looked. There was a stripe across the chest that brought the lifeless form even closer to some existing memory in his brain. He stared at the face in the near total darkness. Its features remained shrouded in grayness and non-formation. Hours went by, and now Jorge's face remained fixed in a stare, looking at the shroud of gray around that face. The shroud was lighter now, and the movement of the sun – far away from his cold prison – let its light filter through more fully. The shroud melted away, and the facial features now presented themselves in recognizable form to Jorge. Jorge's eyes now focused on eyes that could no longer focus themselves. Finally, Jorge spoke, and his own words startled him. "I didn't really mean all that crap about you're going to hell, Justo. I'm really sorry about that."

Sergeant Steve

Sergeant Steve Tasker slipped behind the wheel of the police cruiser. He had decided to keep the trip out of his regular paperwork. It was likely just going to be an unnecessary bother for an innocent citizen, but he had decided to check out the license number in spite of his doubts. If it meant that little Lucy would get straight and use her real name all of the time, then it would be worth it. Maybe this Jorge guy had what it took. The guard at the gate asked him his business, and then waved him over to a parking space outside of the gate.   "Mr. Johnson will be here to answer your questions in a minute." When Johnson arrived, he had Jimmy in tow.

"Sorry to bother you. I know you're busy people." "I have a complaint that I'm following up on. " The patrolman looked at his paper. It was a copy of the vehicle license registration for license number ZRN5264. "I received a complaint from a young woman who said that she witnessed two people tying up a third person, and then putting him into the rear of an SUV with the plate number ZRN5264. I ran the plates for this paper work." The officer waved the paper in the air. "It lists your company as owner of the vehicle. Do you have this vehicle on your property?" Then, in a moment that took sergeant Tasker by surprise, the two men exchanged looks. The surprise for the sergeant wasn't that the men looked at each other. It was the way that they did. The sergeant had been on the force for thirty years. Retirement was not that far off for him. But, in all those years, he had learned to gauge first reactions. What was normal. What was not. His demeanor changed. "What do you say about what I just said?" asked the officer. Johnson shrugged, "I don't have a clue what to make of it officer. Really, we've not kidnapped anyone."

The officer followed the two others to the place, inside the gate, where the SUV was parked. "Do you mind if I look inside of it?" Johnson threw up his hands. "We have nothing to hide officer. Have at it."

The officer made a routine inspection of the vehicle, walking around it and then to the driver's side door. He opened it and slipped behind the wheel. Then he pulled his clipboard up and pulled out a pen. "Just going to make a short report here. I don't really see anything here." Under his breath, he muttered "yet." Then, to the twosome, he said "It'll be just a few minutes." The sergeant waited until Jimmy and Johnson started to express disinterest. His writings on the clipboard had been bogus scribbles, but now the officer began writing down street intersections, dates, and times. The little Trip Tracker navigation unit was mounted low in the vehicle, so it was fairly easy to manage the screen on it without undue notice. Tasker knew that recent state law had made the road history read-outs on navigation units fair game if, and only if, the officer had been granted access to the vehicle itself. Trying to be discrete, he stopped at the three day mark.

The sergeant flipped the first sheet back down onto the clipboard and climbed out of the vehicle. "That should do it" he said. As Johnson led the way back to the gate, he inquired, "Do we get a copy of your report officer?" The officer turned to the man, "Well, I make notes in the field, and then prepare the full report when I get back to my desk. You can get a copy from the department in a couple days. OK?" "Guess so," replied R.M.

As the sergeant got back into the patrol car, his thoughts were on another, separate track relative to where they had been on the incoming trip. He realized that he had made some assumptions about Maria's complaint, jumping to the conclusion that she misinterpreted the situation. He had made a poor decision, from a detective's point of view. He always considered himself a pretty good detective, although he had never been promoted to one. He knew now that he should have asked for a "tail set-up" on Johnson and his buddy, the always smiling fellow. What was his name – Jimmy? Yeah, Jimmy seemed like the untrustworthy type, in the sergeant's opinion. But then, he rationalized, it was fairly unlikely that his boss would go for a tail based upon only Maria's complaint. In the eyes of the department, she would be seen as the untrustworthy one. Sergeant Tasker shook his head. Yes, he had probably managed to fumble through the situation, but in retrospect, he thought, he had gone with the right idea. Lucky for Lucy.

The sergeant's desk was always a mess, and he had a lot of the regular stuff to do. The regular stuff never ended with any improvement, as far as he could ever tell. Maria was different, and he knew he could make a difference. The first step for these people began with making them care about themselves, and sometimes that happened only after they cared for somebody else. Tasker swept the regular stuff off into a box he found perched on top of file holder thirteen. Then, he laid his scribbles out on the desk.

"Lucinda" rang back into Tasker's ear after he dialed the cell number. "It's *Maria*, Lucinda," the sergeant scolded. "Sorry, sergeant Steve." "Anyway, I have run the tag through the registration system, and I've done a little other work related to your complaint – you know – about your Jorge. I've got a few locations that perhaps relate to the situation, and I'd like to read them out to you. If any of them sound like anything you heard from your *boyfriend*, I want you to say so. OK?"

"OK."

The sergeant read through the list, and when he was done, the other end of the connection remained silent. After a little while, she said "We didn't really talk much." Tasker held back a laugh. "I know about the old quarry. I used to go swimming out there when I was a kid. Mom couldn't afford to send me to the pay-for pools. But ... none of the other things you said are familiar to me. And I know Jorge didn't mention any of them ... not even the quarry. "OK kid, I'll see what I can do." He hung up the phone, a little disappointed that Maria could offer no help. The quarry entries were interesting, though. The old swimming hole was no longer used for anything – he knew. It had been closed up for a long while. So, why would these fellows have made two separate trips out there? He mused, it's out there and away from pretty much everything else. Seems like a good place to do something you want to keep on the down-low. Tasker kicked his office chair back, putting his hands behind his head.

Off Blotter

"That old trailer needs to be taken away," thought Steve Tasker as he pulled past it on the stone lane. It's only good for attracting the rats now. Like Maria, he had fond memories attached to the concession items that he once purchased there, when the old man and his wife ran the place. He drove past the old quarry, and up the hill next to it, and down the other side of it. His thoughts continued ... "The old building should go the way of the old trailer."

The officer parked his cruiser on the grass next to the small, but weed overgrown lot adjacent to the building. "It's time to practice being that detective I'm never going to be." Tasker climbed out of the cruiser and walked over to the parking lot. He walked along, side stepping the tall and the short weeds on the outer portion of the lot. As he neared the building, he paused. The weeds were tamped down in two narrow ruts, obviously made by a vehicle. Then he thought *vehicles*. There were numerous tracks there within twenty feet of the lane side of the old building. Tasker moved around to the front of the building, and he stood next to the old freight delivery door, and he saw that it was about half the size that would be needed for any kind of vehicle. It was both locked and cabled. Now Tasker noticed the tracks leading up to the door. Double tracks, he thought. A truck had backed up here, probably. It crossed his mind that the people at the construction firm could own this building now. He chided himself for not checking on that line of information. Tasker considered that the old place could be convenient as a storage facility. Nothing large could go into it probably, but it was an idea that had merit. Tasker, once again, began backing down on his suspicions.

Not one to do anything half-assed, he walked around the rest of the building. Sergeant Tasker was a very thorough police officer. That was why – unbeknownst to him – he really had been considered for a detective's position, in spite of his lack of formal education.

The rear of the old structure once contained a series of windows, but now they were all closed off with bricks. Realizing that remote country places like this old building would be vulnerable to break-ins by vandals, the bricks didn't really surprise the sergeant. Still, he was disappointed that he couldn't put his suspicions, now diminished significantly, entirely to bed. As he walked back to the cruiser, he noticed a vent above the last window on the rear of the old edifice, near the gravel lane. Conveniently, there was a pipe – perhaps an old gas line – that ran along the bottom of the window. Perhaps, he thought, he might grab a peek at the contents of the building, so as to put his last doubts to rest. Tasker was no longer the most nibble of persons, but with some extra noise coming from his mouth in addition to his breath, he managed to climb up onto the pipe. Disappointment followed, because the vents were closed – rusted into position – and he could not budge them. Just then his nostrils caught a bit of something they didn't like. Something really wrong. His interest regained, Tasker pulled at the louvers more vigorously. He took a glove from his pocket and put it on. Then, he grabbed onto the top of the vent, and let all his weight bear on the thing. Tasker had the weight to bear. Begrudgingly, the vent broke loose and pulled out to the open position. Now Tasker's nostrils were in full retreat. The obnoxious smell closed off his windpipe as if by clasping it. "Oh my ..." Tasker thought about rats, hundreds of decaying rats. But no, this was much worse than little rats. This was wrong, foul and wrong. If it were dead rats, then they were giant ones.

Tasker jumped down off of the pipe, making extra sounds over the top of his breath when he hit the ground. "This is a job for *Suzie B*." he muttered to himself. His sweetheart back at the station, Suzie Bablione was the go-to person for answers needed to any questions posited by a patrolman, or detective, or sergeant out on the beat - out in the field. The nature of his question was simple. "Who owns this stinking place?"

He pulled out his service phone, but then stopped before he had pressed any buttons. Today was Suzie's day off, and the person who replaced her on such days – Juanita – was someone he preferred not to deal with. He walked back to the patrol car, and he slipped into the seat. Bringing up the computer console, he tried to log in. "Out of range" came back on the console. "Idiot contractors strike again." he exclaimed to no one. "I can use my civilian level cheap-phone, but not the super-duper three patrolmen's salary priced police department system. As usual."

Sergeant Tasker caught the top of the black SUV out of the corner of his eye, as the fast moving truck popped up over the top of the little ridge. For an instant, he thought it might be Lieutenant Davis's SUV. Then it occurred to him that he had kept the details of the Maria project off of his blotter and his computer account. As the truck came down the incline of the ridge, a man's head could be seen above the roof of the truck. The man was sitting on top of the door holding onto the antenna of the truck with one hand. Instinctively, Tasker went for his sidearm and pulled it from its holster. He swung his right hand and the barrel of the gun quickly around, twisting his body in the seat as he did. On impact, his weapon flew from his hand and bounced on the compacted stones, coming to rest under some weeds. The bullet hit him in the left eye, exited his right ear, and with a dull cracking sound, the flattened piece of metal shattered a small half dollar sized piece of windshield. Finally, it ricocheted onto the floor. The mortally wounded policeman slumped over, and rolled out onto the stones.

The two men from the black SUV went into frantic high-speed mode, with one of them opening the freight door while the other dragged the body of the dead policeman in the direction of the opening.   The second man pulled the dead weight of sergeant Tasker across the threshold of the freight door and dropped him inside the threshold.   The two men returned to the SUV, and walked around to the back of the truck.   They pulled a large Tyvek bag from the truck and then another one. Both bags, they dropped onto the stones.   Each of the men took a bag, pulling the lumpy dead weights across the gravel towards the freight door.   They struggled with the bags, as they were filled with rigid forms that twisted back and forth in the bags as they were pulled along the stone pathway. The two bags were placed in front of the cooler.   One man took keys from his pocket and opened the cooler.   Once opened, the other man pulled Jorge from the cooler.   When this man saw that Jorge had managed to get loose of his hand ties, he retied them.   This was done without any fuss, as the mexican was weak and nearly unconscious from dehydration.

After driving the patrol car up to the edge of the quarry, Slith pushed it in.

Both men ran to the area, inside the building, where the gasoline containers were kept.   There was one particular container marked with a big black X. "We want to be clear of this place when the flames hit this can Slith. It'll be pretty to watch.   Remember what a pint of it did to the pip squeak's apartment?   This is nearly five gallons!   It's gonna be the Fourth of July."   The smaller one smiled. "And I didn't bring any beer and popcorn – damn it."   The men made sure to douse the unprocessed ones heavily with the gasoline, and then Slith carefully placed the X marked container in the doorway of the cooler. "They won't even find the bones. It's both incendiary and explosive."   The bigger of the two men hauled the body of the unfortunate patrolman over to the cooler, and laid him next to the X can. The two Tyvec bags were already there.   Slith kicked the bag closest to the X can. The unclosed end opened, and smiling Jimmy's head fell with a dull thud onto the concrete floor. Slith noticed that his mouth was open and his teeth showing. "He died like he lived." Both men laughed, and then from the larger of the two came the words: "Let's blow this joint!"   Slith reached down, saying "Wait! The big boss wants this one for some reason."   Slith grabbed Jorge by the belt and began to drag him across the floor.   Finally, at the truck, the Mexican was hoisted and shoved unceremoniously into the vehicle.

The SUV pulled out of the drive and then just off to the side of the road in front of the quarry.   The occupants could see neither smoke nor flame over the top of the ridge.   Finally, Slith said,   "We'll give it a minute or two." The concussion of the blast ripped long shards of aluminum from the side of the trailer.   Several pieces of brick shrapnel nailed the side of the black SUV as the blast wave rocked it violently.   The driver kicked down the pedal and the truck launched back out onto the road.

Hell

Lieutenant Davis stood next to the quarry as the tow truck pulled the unfortunate sergeant Tasker's patrol car from the water.   Detective Warner was standing next to him. He looked at Davis, "It wasn't as deep here - on the end of the lagoon - as they thought." Davis shook his head up and down, "They left the top half of the car's windows sticking out of the water. They couldn't see through the muck well enough to determine that the old quarry lagoon had a shallow end. After it went in, there was nothing they could do."

Warner returned, "Guess that's lucky for our investigation, but

BEELZEBUB'S BARGAIN

not so lucky for poor Steve. The guy was one of a kind. Suzie thinks he was doing a little off the board work to help straighten out a young woman he had arrested – I guess on several occasions – for solicitation. Her name was "Lucinda" on the street, but really *Maria* somebody. We're trying to locate her now." Davis looked up reflectively, "Well, that assumes she's not lying somewhere in this mess." Davis and Warner turned around to look at the X can's havoc and destruction. "A little bit of Armageddon here Lieutenant." "No doubt. Had to be military grade stuff. It's fascinating how that cooler melted down, but all of these body parts are still pretty much intact. Charred, but identifiable." The police crews were working the site, carefully photographing the various body parts where they lay. All of the city's crime scene investigators had been called to the scene, and they were meticulously collecting the evidence of what surely would go down as the most horrific crime to ever have been visited upon the city. One of the investigators walked up to Davis, holding a bag. The charred service weapon was only half the width that its manufacturer had originally made it. Its Kevlar reinforced handle grips were gone, and the steel underneath it had flowed out into an artistic pattern – like decorative wrought iron leaves. "Where did you find it?" The investigator pointed to the spot, only twenty five feet from an area of the building that was now mostly gone – but that was indicated, on fire department drawings, as having been a freight door.

"So, it looks like Tasker had drawn his weapon. Apparently, too late." Warner observed. "There was no body in the cruiser." The two superior officers now walked towards the still smoking building, and then across the charred foundation in the area where the door had been. One of the firemen, who was also an arson investigator, stood next to the cooler. It's cool enough to walk over here fellas – just don't touch any metal. That is still pretty hot." The men walked around the cooler. Warner pointed at the excavations where the bones had been removed. Only one body had been found there, at the entry door to the cooler. With three quarters of the walls melted down, the bottom of the cooler was plainly visible in the strong sunlight. "Don't know how many bodies that adds up to yet," said the fireman, pointing to a pile of mostly disintegrated stick-like pieces of material that - here and there – retained the telltale markings of bones. Davis commented, "Maybe four ... three or four ..." "It's pretty hard to tell how much was completely vaporized. The explosives, like I said, must have been some kind of military grade incendiary ... I've never seen anything like it." Warner agreed.

Davis turned, thinking he would get a look at some of the other evidence being collected on the outer boundaries of the crime scene – now covering several acres. As he turned, he caught a glimpse of metal in the ash. He reached for a towel from his back pocket, then reached down and picked up the shiny oblong piece of metal. Although it was melted completely flat, its shape and a few hints of detail gave it away. Warner frowned, "The sergeant's badge."

Long way home

Valerie slumped in the chair. Mr. B stood next to the table, leaning up against it. "Where is Miguel?" Valerie shook her head, "I've got only one way to say it, and it doesn't matter how many times you ask. He dumped me when he figured out that I was a snitch for you people. That's all. I haven't seen him since then." Mr. B produced a wry smile, "You're holding up pretty well, Valerie. But, you forget that we have recordings of everything he said to you, and everything you said to him in the apartment and in his car. That includes everything you said to each other in bed. It's what happens when you keep your cell phone on the night stand. That's just an FYI for you – for future reference. As a result of this, we know you fell in love with him, and that, of course, you will not give him up willingly." The tall form moved closer to Valerie. "Being aware of this, I went through the drill anyway, just to hear what I knew I would hear." Mr. B sat down next to Valerie, scanning her shapely figure from top to bottom. Valerie shuddered.

"We are a drug company, you know. Maybe, not in the conventional sense are we one, but we do know a great deal about drugs. We have created chemicals for many unique purposes. Generally speaking, these are not of a conventional nature. We have created a series of very interesting drugs, all leading up to one which – I tell you this in all seriousness – will allow us to take control of this planet. Complete control. No person, anywhere, in any country, will be immune to its effects. But, that's not of immediate interest. My immediate interest is more acutely tied to you and what you know. What we will soon know." Mr. B stood up, and stepped back. "Gerald!" The door opened, and a man came in through the door of the room. The man held a syringe full of a reddish fluid. Mr. B waved his hand in the direction of Valerie. "Gerald, here is our patient."

Gerald approached Valerie, and as he did, the latter stood up and backed into a corner of the room. The tall man pursued her into the corner, and as the back of her head hit the wall, she grabbed her attacker's arm and pushed back against it. Gerald was at least twice her size. A short tussle ensued, and Gerald managed to twist one of her arms behind her back, and simultaneously inject half the load of the syringe into her other arm. Valerie closed her eyes as tightly as she could, while twisting her body with all her might. She managed to break

Gerald's hold on the syringe, but her efforts were to no avail. Gerald pulled Valerie's arm backwards until she was once again in a straight up position, spun her face-first against the wall, and held her there. With the fiercest portion of her strength lost, she was helpless. Gerald put firm pressure on the plunger, and pushed the full dose of the reddish fluid into the hapless woman's arm. Keeping her arm pinned behind her back, Gerald maneuvered the woman across the room and back down into the chair. Now, Valerie was crying. She moved her gaze from Gerald to Mr B., and back again. "So, how long do I have to live?" Mr. B. laughed, "It's not going to kill you Valerie. It's just a little catalyst to make you more cooperative. We like that word in chemistry. We use catalysts for most everything, and now we have given you a very special one." "It will help you to be more honest with us."

Valerie now looked at Mr. B. "What have you done to my mother, you bastard?" The wry smile came back to the tall figure's face. "Why, Valerie, nothing. Nothing at all. We just needed to convey to you the wisdom of having one last meeting with us. Your mother still sits there in the asylum, and she still rocks in her rocking chair, all day long. Just the same as she has done for years, Valerie. Our people at the asylum take very good care of her. It's nothing for you to fret about."

Shroud

Miguel picked his way around the largest of the blackish rivers of sludge-like material. He paused in front of the black plastic shroud, waiting for Domingo to reach him. "3C" was marked on the tag hanging inside a plastic pouch attached to the left corner post of the stall. Miguel touched Domingo on the shoulder as he came close. Then he nodded at the rotating camera, hanging above them, from a long pole dropped down from the ceiling. Domingo whispered, "I've seen surprisingly few of those Miguel. They don't expect people to get inside of this place." Domingo mimicked Miguel's earlier gallows grin, saying "no one in their right minds would be here." None of the orderlies – the body handlers, or whatever else one might call them – wore uniforms, so the two intruders had a reasonable chance to blend in with the environment.

Miguel pulled the black shroud aside, as he and Domingo slipped into the little space. The men stood there, inside of the stall, for several minutes. Neither moved anything other than eyes, two pairs of which now observed the scene, trying to comprehend it. The lighting was poor, but for the two men standing there, it was not poor enough. Finally, Domingo let go with "Jesus."

Miguel's face was drawn up and twisted into a squint of disbelief. "It's breathing." The form was that of a human. There were two arms and two legs. There was an area above the torso that seemed to be a head. The body was lashed in several places with nylon strapping. These straps held the body close to the metal beneath it – which the twosome observed to be a thin layer of aluminum sheeting mounted on a steel frame. The metal bed was tilted, and a hole could be seen on the low end. The smelly, malignant mass of puss and blood streamed out of various parts of this poor human. It drained slowly, dripping down, creating little blackish brown rippled tracks in several places. The ooze slowly made its way to the low end of the steel bed, and pooled there. A slow swirl of this lipid mass drained from the pool, through the hole, and then down onto the concrete floor below. Just as was the case with the drainage tile, the edge of the hole sprouted formations of reddish-black-brown icicles, dangling six inches below it.

Atop the torso, where the head of a human would normally be, could be seen a bulbous collection of what might have been accurately described as giant boils. The boil-like projections were six or seven inches across, and the skin was stretched tightly over them. There were lesions in the skin there, where it had stretched too tightly, and where it had gone beyond its elastic limit. In those places the skin had burst open, ripping jagged lines, dripping more of the grisly liquid, and adding to the pool on the metal bed. Miguel and Domingo took all of this in, but now they both looked at the same spot. Neither man could speak. On the left side of the area where the head should have been, something moved. The scarring and deformation had hidden it until it moved, and now it moved back and forth between Miguel and Domingo. Looking at one, and then the other. It was alive, and it could see.

Now there was a noise, startling both men. "This way, Miguel!" Domingo led his friend back towards the rear corner of the room. Then, in a low tone of voice, "I have a theory." Domingo whisked into stall *8D*, and held the shroud aside for Miguel. Once again, the two men absorbed the gruesome scene inside the stall. Once again, they each remained silent, as their eyes sent to their brains images that were both gory and complicated at the same time. Finally, Miguel blew out a slow breath, and looked at Domingo, "I'm with your theory Domingo. Exactly. This is an assembly line process of the most unimaginable sort. A macabre sort of inhumanity visited upon our innocent brothers for the purpose of growing something in them ... for what evil purpose I can't even begin to think about, or to guess about." The body on the metal sheet was lashed, like the others, but there were fewer projections under the skin.

Miguel pointed at the only remaining boil-like mass on the body - where it hung off of the side of the abdomen. It was obvious to the two men that this body's potential had been nearly spent. There were a half dozen poorly stitched scars on it, including one that had pulled the face askew. It had, in a way, morphed the unfortunate man's face into a sort of leather handbag, with the skin stitched down over the place where the eye socket should have been. Domingo pulled his prayerbook, and read a few lines "May the good Lord correct this terrible thing, and may this man find his heaven." He turned to look at Miguel. "He's dead." "They grew these things ... these boils ... or whatever they are ..." Domingo reached down and touched the cold flesh in the area of the only remaining protrusion. He pinched it slightly. "You know what I think, Miguel?" Miguel shrugged. "I think these are cancerous tumors."

"They won't be back here again until they take away the body, and so we're probably OK for a bit." The commotion picked up, and now a man could be heard cursing and swearing. The noise of the cursing man got louder and louder, and it occurred to Domingo that they were coming to stall 8D. The tense twosome stood there – as straight up rigid as the body lying on the steel platform. The shuffling feet stopped short of 8D. There was a sound – one that carried trouble in the noise. The dull thud was followed by the sound of something being dragged . The twosome stood there for five minutes, waiting for the sounds to end with footsteps leading away from the room. Miguel's eyes went wild - "Valerie could be in here!" Instantly, he whipped back the plastic shroud. Now, in a desperate search, he went from stall to stall pulling back the black plastic from each one, every time doing so with his heart in his throat. Domingo followed, hoping that the noise would not be noticed, but realizing that stealth was now far beyond the ability of his friend. At last, they had covered the space, from end to end. Relieved that she was not among the victims, but sickened by what they had seen, they retreated to one of the empty rooms.

Truth Serum

Mr. B and Gerald had left Valerie alone in the nearly empty room. She had tried the door to no avail, and had finally resigned herself to sit in the chair, and to empty her mind. Too much had happened. What was this fluid that now ran in her veins? If it were a truth serum, like sodium pentathol, wouldn't it wear off in a couple hours? It seemed to Valerie that she had already been in the room for that much time. She had practiced emptying her mind, to prepare for the interrogation. Could she deny them? She had her doubts. These people had the stuff, no doubt, to make her talk. How could she live with herself if she betrayed Miguel and the others? All these questions filtered through her mind, again and again.

Finally, when the door did open, Mr. B walked in. He was accompanied by two of the orderlies. "Come, Valerie. We are going to take a tour." Valerie glared back, "That was *some* truth serum you gave me. I feel perfectly normal." Mr. B smiled, "Well, if you want that old time stuff, I can give it to you. It'll make you sick, and we will get some unreliable information. We have a better way. Please, now come along with us. Jonesy and William here are eager to show you a few things. " The foursome walked out into the hall. They walked down two different long corridors, and then turned into a large room with a concrete floor and unpainted cinder-block walls. The orderlies took Valerie first to *2B*, and then to *2C*, but Valerie was vomiting already inside of the first stall. The orderlies dragged her through the tour, forcing her to witness the grim scene within each successive stall.

"You animals!" she screamed at William as he shoved her

under the shroud of stall *2D*. Mr. B grasped Valerie by both shoulders, and shook her, "Come now, we're nearly done here. This is maybe the worst of the worst in stall "*2C*" Valerie. I think that our tour has served its purpose, and it should have been more than enough to convince you to do exactly what it is you must do." "What the hell is wrong with you people, she half screamed and half sobbed. You ... you beasts of hell ... you sadistic bastards!"

Valerie found herself sitting in the same chair, back in the room with the desk and the bad memory of Gerald and his syringe. Valerie was still sobbing as she looked up to see Mr. B leaning against the desk. "You're insane!" she screamed. You're utterly insane!"

Mr. B shook his head. "No Valerie, I'm not insane. I'm bringing to this world what it has wanted for centuries, and what it has dreamed of for centuries. I'm doing what no one else would do. I'm doing the hard part that no one could do, thanks to their morality or their laws. I'm shedding those things ... to do what no man has ever done before .. to bring a benefit to mankind like none before. Someday, they'll erect statues in my honor Valerie." Valerie shook her head, "No you insane murderer. You insane homicidal lunatic. I'm sure that those people will feel the same as I do: disgusted by your sickness."

Mr. B's smile waned. "Valerie, my dear, you are about to witness first hand the glory of my discovery. You see, we did the hard thing to do. When you use rats, you don't get to the source of the problem because ... well, rats are different than people. We solved that problem with the illegal immigrants. They were convenient, because with them we didn't need to be bothered by ... those troublesome views of morality and those laws that would have stopped us. We needed hundreds of people, and their absence would have been noticed. But – the illegals never existed to start with! We were careful to select those that had few or no entanglements with others, with loved ones, and so forth. We made accommodations."

"You're a pig," spat Valerie. Mr. B ignored her and kept on, "We found, in the first hundred, a very special substance when we analyzed the tumors. We were amazed to find that this substance – when it was put in combination with some of our brilliant chemistry – cured cancer! It cured the cancer completely, with never a remission! Ever! With chemical modification, this wonderful substance cured the tumors it came from! Can you imagine? But, we had a problem. The problem was that very little of this substance was to be found in each tumor. We needed large tumors, and we needed many of them, and we needed to be able to grow them quickly. Otherwise, we couldn't have the cure. Of course we sacrificed a few people. How could we not?"

Mr. B paused. Then he began again, "We needed to create the worst cancer ever ... the fastest growing ... the most aggressive ... and we did it Valerie! With the help of those few hundreds of illegals, we created the most aggressive cancer on earth. Why? To have the cure! Of course!" Now Mr. B had raised his voice. The glee in his voice came across to Valerie, and it made her shudder. She knew, without a doubt, that Mr. B was completely insane. "You know Valerie, that I ... well ... my silent partners and I ... will be compensated handsomely for this. Why shouldn't we be?Like I said, we did the hard work, we took the chances. We shall have the rewards! Around here, we call the cure *The Drug*. Of course, it's *The Drug*. Of every concoction ever invented or discovered by any scientist in this or any century, what would be the most befitting of the term, *The Drug*? The cure for cancer, Valerie. What else?"

Mr. B paused again. He seemed to regain his composure. "Of course, we cannot allow anything to stop this important business. Your little group puts our operation at risk, and that is not acceptable. That is why, Valerie, Gerald had to give you the other drug, the one that causes the aggressive cancer, the one that we gave to all of those in the stalls ... in *2B* and *2C* and *2D*. "

Valerie's face assumed the look of abject horror. An ice cold stabbing fear ran down her spine. "You ... you did that to me? You gave me what they have?" She half stood up from her chair, pushing herself up with trembling hands, but immediately collapsed onto the floor, sobbing. The orderlies pulled her back into the chair. "Now now Valerie, it's not so bad. Like I said, we have the drug to cause the most malignant cancer ever known. But, we have the cure! It's pretty simple Valerie. You give us Miguel and the others, we give you the cure, and you live. Otherwise, you die. I assure you Valerie, it's not the way you want to die."

The Shelf

One of the investigators tapped Davis on the shoulder. "I have something I want you to see." Davis waved to Warner, and the two men followed the investigator over the low ridge and down to the spot where the sergeant's patrol car had been pulled. The once white car was now a ruddy brown, as the sediment in the water made it look like a junkyard castoff. Streaks of the sediment had made little designs on the sides of the vehicle. "It was when we pulled the car out that we noticed it." The investigator pointed to a series of whitish brown, stick-like pieces that formed a sort of pathway out of the quarry. These pieces were scattered around the two ruts leading to the front of the patrol car. A small pile of these things remained lodged behind the car's front tire, away from the water. Warner stared in amazement. "Bones." The investigator's right cheekbone pulled up now, clearly showing his disgust for the discovery. "It's why the car didn't sink." Davis stood there for a full fifteen seconds, hearing what his investigator said, but not believing. The investigator turned and shouted to a man standing on the edge of the quarry, but a couple hundred feet closer to the road. "Come here Mike!"

Mike pulled the scuba tank from his back, and now he fast stepped in the direction of his super. At last, when the wet suit clad man reached the three of them, crime scene supervisor Smitty spoke, "Mike, tell the detective here what you saw." "Well, of course we were looking for debris and ... you know ... body parts in the quarry. That's sorta my specialty. I've been doing it a long time but ..." Mike took a deep breath and released it. "Never anything like this. We found a few pieces of evidence, and small pieces out in the middle, but then when Smitty here saw the bones come up with the car, I went down to have a look. I couldn't see that far in the water – thanks to it's being stirred up by the retrieval of the poor sergeant's vehicle, so we brought in some high powered underwater lighting gear. With that, I could see plenty. The light was good for ... maybe six or eight feet, and -" Mike paused. "It was surreal – I mean crazy surreal. Like some kinda *bad B movie* or something. "

Mike paused again. "I couldn't believe it was real. I started swimming, and the light kept showing me the same thing. I'm not sure how far out I went, but it could have been forty feet. That's where the bone field stopped, because that's the real edge of the quarry. It goes down a couple hundred feet, at least, and I couldn't dive it with just this wet suit ... you know ... too much pressure. We've sent a request back to the station to find a contractor, so they can use their high pressure diving suits for this." Smitty pointed Mike in the direction of the group he had been working with, saying "Thanks. You can go back to what you were doing." Mike nodded and started walking back along the edge of the quarry. Smitty turned to Warner, "These are some of the underwater shots. As you can see, they are a bit blurry, but they show it well enough." Warner took the freshly printed photos from Smitty's hand.

Davis and Warner went back to the scene of the demolished building. "What do you think this is all about?" Warner's face was blank. "Holocaust, the sequel? I mean, I don't know what to say. I'm calling the feds in on this. This is no longer a city, or county, or even a state level crime. This is going to be news in Bangladesh and in Hong Kong. Mafia? This is some kind of dumping yard for mass murder, but it's no serial killing misogynist piling up this many bones. It's entirely crazy. I mean, I want to have those bones checked in the lab, and have the lab guy tell me they're all fake, and it's just a big damned joke. But ... this battleground we've been working on all day is no joke. It's a reality check. I'm afraid it makes the bones real – lab or no lab."

Davis's look was as blank as Warner's. "There were a couple hundred bodies in those photos if there was one. Damn!" "G-- damned insanity!" Davis picked up his cell phone and dialed the chief's number. After a short conversation, the chief agreed with Davis about the whole matter. The chief had already been apprised of the situation, in general, and had been sent photos of the grisly quarry scene. In this particular instance, for once, the three patrolman's salary communication system had worked.

As he disconnected from the chief, Davis knew that his boss

would soon be dialing *the number*, the number he never really wanted to call. It just ran against the grain to give up your jurisdiction. It was the last thing the chief, or for that matter, Davis himself would do, under any circumstances that he could imagine. These circumstances were beyond the imaginations of either of them.

Near Morgue

Miguel and Domingo left the near-morgue and quickly retreated into the first empty room, next to the door they had first used to gain entry. Domingo commented, "I don't need to see any more of this."

They found a little notch in the cinder-block wall. It seemed to be a place that would not warrant an accidental visit by any of the morgue keepers. The two of them sat, just behind the little notch, and Miguel pulled the sealed plastic bag from his pants pocket. Miguel had miniaturized the fire department drawings, and now the two men scrutinized them. After a while Miguel looked up at Domingo. "This place is only for the awful things the Stasi are doing down the corridor. They're growing these tumors – why?" Domingo shrugged, "Can't fathom. It seems that if they were testing some formula for reducing them, they wouldn't need so many victims. Also, the progression of the "assembly line" process, so to speak, seems not to diminish the size of the tumors at all." Miguel shook his head in agreement, "I have the feeling that these things are used – processed in some way – maybe to extract something from the tumors themselves. If that is true, then there must be some other facility where this is done. I have seen almost nothing in this building to support any kind of processing whatsoever." Miguel pointed to the miniaturized blueprint of the two company buildings. "We are here, in building A", he said. "I suspect that any processing operation might happen in building B. Naturally, they would separate the two parts of the operation – because the psychopathic lunatics who are the type of people who could ever be convinced to work in this environment must be a rare breed. Maybe the head psychopaths recruit in the prisons, and look for killers. I dunno ... " Miguel continued, "There are a few crazies working in this building. The other side of things ... the extraction and processing operations ... must be much more labor intensive. It is likely that they bring in people who are not so depraved as those who work the beds. They need skilled people."

Domingo nodded, "Those on the other side could be told, I suppose, that the tumors are grown in cows or sheep or whatever ..."

Miguel again moved his hand over the plastic sheathed paper ... "I've been looking at this blueprint, and I've noticed that building A was mapped out originally as being just for storage purposes. But ... there is a line drawing here-" Miguel pointed at a spot on the paper, "-where I think there may be a tunnel. That's probably what is used to transport the material to building B." Domingo frowned, "So - the tunnel - it'll have some serious security due to the type of people who likely work on the other side."

"No doubt Domingo. They'll be heavily armed – on this side. The other side surely will seem more innocuous, but won't be." Domingo looked down. He pulled his prayerbook from his pocket and slapped it on his knee. "Miguel, we're a couple of mexican guys with no guns. You know, I've never had one in my hand, being always a sort of pacifist. I wouldn't know how to use one really. I'd shoot myself in the foot. What the hell are we doing here?" Miguel looked serious. "I really don't know if I can believe all of this. Really, I wish somebody would just wake me up. I wish the damned alarm clock would go off so that I could hit the snooze button and go back to my extra ten minute nap. I'd just lie there, thinking about how great it was that it had all been a bad dream. You ever done that Domingo?"

"I don't dream. They say people who don't dream have something wrong with them. Is there something wrong with me Miguel?" Miguel's face blanked, "There's probably something wrong with both of us for being here. But, somebody's gotta stop these people. We could go back down that stinking drain pipe, and turn ourselves in to the authorities. We could tell them a story they wouldn't believe. We could show them these photos." Miguel tapped the digital camera in his breast pocket. "But, then what? These photos are real, but they are so grotesque that they wouldn't be believed. They'll think we are playing a ghoulish Halloween game. Then we'd be nowhere but in detention, awaiting deportation. Maybe that would be better. Maybe the U.S. ain't so grand, after all. Maybe it's their damned problem. Maybe I'll forget all about them, go back to Mexico and take up drinking Tequila." Domingo looked at his friend, "And, they'll just go on killing our people?" Miguel shrugged. "You know how many of us die doing the dirty work in this country. This kind of thing is probably the tip of the iceberg, really. We "don't exist", so when we disappear, nobody notices. It's too convenient. Bad people – evil people – will always take advantage of such a thing."

Miguel paused and then with his voice lowered, he said "They could have Valerie. I hope not, but I can't quit this business until I know what happened to her. So ... I can't just crawl back down the pipe, and go home."

"Miguel, how do we get to the tunnel from here?"

"We don't, Domingo. Like you said, they will have who knows what ... uzis maybe ... at the entrance to the tunnel, or along inside it somewhere. I doubt there's a way we are going to get through that tunnel undetected. We need not to be caught. We get caught and this atrocity goes on and on. One of us needs to go back out of the drain, and take these photos to the authorities. Maybe they'll believe it. Maybe they won't. You need to go back out of the drain Domingo." Miguel handed the camera over to Domingo, and then slowly breathed out the words, "I'm going to look for Valerie ..."

Bad Memory Room

The room filled with the bad memories of Gerald's syringe had become Valerie's little jail. Occasionally there was the orderly with water or with food. Every time he came, she jumped in her skin as the noisy keys rattled in the lock of the steel door. Mostly what he brought were dry and tasteless packaged snack items or overly sweet fare of the type meant for vending machines. There was little to do but to think, but Valerie didn't want to think. Thinking meant filling her conscious thoughts with Gerald and stalls 2B and 2C. She wanted to force all of that out of her mind. She wanted to think happy thoughts – thoughts about her mother before she was committed, and thoughts about Miguel. She sat there, smiling and thinking about how it had been with Miguel, and how he had waved off her betrayal. She had little choice in the matter of Peterson, of course – the sadistic bastards would have made short work of her mother in the asylum. Valerie's smile faded. Miguel didn't know the details of her ordeal.

She had only bad choices from which to choose, and she beat herself, mentally, for making the worst one. Or was it? She didn't know. Which was worse? She had drawn fire away from Domingo and Miguel and the others. That was something. It wasn't a completely bad choice, then, was it? Maybe, she had saved the others. Her lip stiffened, her face became resolute, and now her thoughts were verbalized into a low whisper, "This time Miguel, *there will be no betrayal.*"

There was noise in the hallway outside of the steel door, a shuffling noise that seemed not to be the orderly. There were two or three distinct voices now, on the other side of it. The noisy lock unlatched and the door opened. Jorge walked into the room. Slith came up immediately behind Jorge and pushed him ahead and into the corner of the room, and then over to the small table there. The two orderlies wrestled the weakened man down onto the table, The steel door opened a little more and then Valerie's face twisted into a mask of revulsion as the unsmiling automaton – the rotten bastard with the reddish fluid and the syringe and the nightmare - entered the room and closed the door behind him. Valerie sat and listened to the spiel one more time. Jorge had already been given the tour, she knew. She didn't need to ask. She could see it in the poor man's eyes.

When it was over, the ugly ones left. There was a moment of silence as the two strangers took each other in. Finally, Jorge spoke. "Who are you?" She sat there with a far away look, unsmiling. "Well, I guess – like you – I'm one of the walking dead." The conversation picked up when Jorge divulged his name. Valerie had heard Domingo say it. She brightened, and so did Jorge, as they came to the realization that they were the same side of things.

Feelings related to putting himself into his perilous situation hadn't yet seeped into Miguel's psyche. That began only after the separation from Domingo. Only then did he begin to feel intimidated by his situation. Even after all that he had seen, Domingo's company had allowed Miguel to repress or deflect the feelings of horror that should have been natural and immediate. Now he needed a weapon ... being without one was suddenly unacceptable. Miguel slipped into the entryway of a small door along the corridor he was navigating. The door had been ajar, and he could see that it contained various things related to cleaning. Once inside, he pulled the door almost to the closed position, reasoning that this might allow for – maybe – a second or two of advance notice when an intruder came through it. He reasoned that he might find a place to hide among the supplies. His mind raced as he took inventory of the items on the supply shelves. He looked for anything he could weaponize. There was a bottle of chlorine bleach, several drain cleaners, and not much else. He picked up one of the drain cleaners and looked at the active ingredient list. Sodium hydroxide might do the trick, he thought – it would be better than bleach. He picked up the next bottle of drain cleaner, turned it over and read the label. "Sulfuric acid" he mumbled to himself. "None of this is good enough to do anything but get me killed quickly," he thought out loud. He blew out a breath of air, and resigned himself to the fact that he would be vulnerable.

Miguel had a problem. The corridors were long and there were very few doors along them. Additionally, the halls were all very straight, with nary a place anywhere that he might hide. There really was no choice, he decided. He would just take his chances. He slipped out of the janitor's supply closet, and turned to his left. Just then he felt a jab to the back of his head. Something cold was being pressed against his temple. "I don't think you belong here," accused the first orderly. The second one walked in front of Miguel, and turned around. Miguel saw the guns and the shoulder holsters that they carried under their smocks, something that - until now, he had not noticed. The second one's weapon had been drawn, and it was pointed at Miguel's head. "You need to come with us."

Jeffry

For lieutenant Davis and captain Warner, the morning of the third day began in the same way as the two before. There was a significant difference; however. Neither one was any longer in charge of the scene. The feds had arrived in a big way. One of the fanciest mobile forensic units in the country was an eighteen wheel, semi-tractor trailer rig that hosted a full forensic laboratory on wheels. This was what the big bucks associated with federal jurisdiction brought to the table, and Warner was pleased to have it. He wasn't particularly pleased about being a spectator.

Much of the collection work had been done by the local and state guys, so the newcomers could focus more closely on pure forensics. Throughout the morning they worked, taking fingerprints and teeth and DNA samples in an attempt to determine who these people were. Jeffry was the fed in charge, and now he and the two local lawmen stood in a group. "Let me bring you up to speed captain Warner, lieutenant Davis. We have much work to do if we are to identify these people. The reason is simple. Initial testing indicates that they were all Hispanics, with the possible exception of two of them. These people may have been undocumented workers, and if that is the case, we may never really identify them." Davis and

Warner nodded slowly, taking in what the fed had to say. Jeffry continued, "There is one thing that will factor into the investigation in a big way. Most of the bodies of the people we found were in serious decay. The human body is a bag of bacteria. Usually, within only a few days time, the decomposition becomes exponential, and the body bloats. Because these bodies had been cooled somewhat – we think the cooler was operational – the decay was ameliorated. My colleagues believe that some or most of the victims had been deceased already for up to two weeks when our little piece of Armageddon came along. That's our best guess, based on everything we have so far."

"Then, there is the issue of the ownership of the land, and of course, the big question about who pays the electric bill for the cooler. Our investigators made pretty quick work out of that – and they determined that an elderly couple has owned the property for about forty five years. The elderly couple remained on power company documents as the responsible party for paying the electric bill, and they paid those bills every month for the renters. In the interview, it was discovered that the arrangement for prepaid electric service was something the renters had specifically asked for and had received, because of an offer to include overly generous monthly estimated prepayment amounts in the rent."

Jeffry paused, "It's obvious that the renters wanted to avoid any connection to the property. Their nefarious purposes for it are now too clear. The couple who owns the property said that the renter always paid with money orders or cash. They said that the money was sent religiously, and was never a day late. In fact, it was usually more than a week early. The mister added the comment that the payments were usually for two or three months at a time, even though that had not been called for in the agreement. It's obvious that the renters didn't want to give the couple much reason to poke around. Add to that the fact that the elderly man is wheelchair bound, and I think we have pretty good evidence that the property was preselected for the indirection it would provide."

"Clever operators," finally came from Warner.

Jeffry continued, "There is another thing my forensic people have discovered about the bodies, gentlemen. It's macabre, to say the least." Jeffry shuffled his feet, making little circles in the dirt with his shoe. Then he looked up. "Many of the bodies, according to my experts over there in the trailer, appear to have been partially dissected prior to the explosion. They can tell this by the decomposition that has occurred in areas that have been ripped open, but that would have been "cleaner", so to speak, if the wounds had been caused by the explosion. It's mighty strange."

Davis spoke, "So ... someone is killing and dissecting Mexican illegal immigrants, and storing them in a cooler until they can be "cleaned", or processed in some way. The processing leaves only bones, and those are dumped into the pond. Good Lord."

Jeffry interjected, "We thought it could be an organ theft ring, at first. Unfortunately, when we took a good look at all of the pieces and parts, we found evidence that the organs that would have been most profitable remained in sufficient quantity to disqualify the theory. It's got me hanging ... not clueless, but hanging. Gentlemen, I must get back at it here ... if you'll excuse me." Jeffry headed off in the direction of the trailer, and Davis and Warner turned in the direction of their cars.

Captain Warner stepped into his office and back into normalcy. Now, he could turn off the bad episode of the twilight zone that had been his place in space for the past three days. There was the lady at the first desk, making a complaint for a dog that bit her son. "He knows it's vicious, and he doesn't do anything about it," she lamented. There on the "hot bench" were two juveniles who had petty theft on their minds at the wrong time. They sat, glum faced, waiting for their mothers or fathers or whatevers.

Ah, and there stood leggy officer Cindi. Miniskirt clad, vice working, leggy officer Cindi. It was on more than one occasion that captain Warner had thoughts related to a nascent fantasy about an officer Cindi who was more vice than cop. But, captain Warner was a married man, and he always pushed those thoughts away appropriately. Well, maybe after a few indulgent seconds he pushed them away. There was a Hispanic in the first interrogation room – not the politically correct term for the room, but the one he used. He was waving his arms and saying something about "it's not being fake". Warner smiled, thinking about what was probably another Mexican guy who picked the wrong chap to laminate his ID cards. Warner walked back to the break room and grabbed a soda from the vending machine. He had just plopped down into a chair when the officer who had been interviewing the Hispanic came back into the room. He was carrying a handful of photos, which he laid down onto the table in front of Warner. "Captain, this guy has some wild eyed story about Mexicans being used to grow tumors which are cut out and used for some unknown reason. He brought these photos with him. Sure as heck he's under the influence of something and pulled these fakes out of a video to make fun of us. That's what I think. Here's his digital camera. He supplied it as 'evidence'." Warner took the camera, and the subordinate cop continued, "Anyway, what's crazy is that he's illegal. So coming in here with the wild eyed story gets him arrested. Go figure." Now, it was captain Warner's turn to be wild eyed. He swept the photos up off of the table, jumped up from his chair, and blurted out "Let's talk to this man!"

Back in his regular cop days, Warner had rocketed through the ranks of the department to become its premiere detective. This was for a reason, but it didn't take Warner's caliber of detective to put these numbers together.

Jeffry noticed the captain's car as it rolled through the stones on the lane, leaving a billowing cloud of dust in the air behind it.   The words "that's some big hurry you're in capitan ..." went through the head of the lead crime scene investigator. Twenty minutes later, there were no longer any questions in Jeffry's mind about the hurry factor that the captain had exhibited. Warner had called ahead to make sure that Jeffry would be there, but he wanted the fed to see the evidence and hear the testimony first hand. Domingo's command of English brought the message home quickly, and for the first fifteen minutes neither lawman said anything. "Let me have the camera" were the first words from Jeffry. He went to the door of the very small office he commanded in the trailer, and called for one of his people. He handed the camera off, saying "I need to know if these are real."   The forensic specialist nodded.   Jeffry turned to the two other occupants of the office, and said "We need to take a road trip."

9

Clean up

T he gate of the stone yard hung open as the trio stepped
through it, and they walked in the direction of the the
office on the end of the building. The guard shack had been
cleaned out, leaving only a few small pieces of the plastic
ribbon material used to seal the top of packs of cigarettes. The
clean spot, where the computer had rested on the counter for
years, was clearly outlined on the otherwise dust encrusted
shelf.

The office door was likewise unguarded and unlocked.
Someone had left in a hurry, but they were very thorough.
Warner began to walk toward a small door, partially open and
hiding a darkened interior. As he tried to push it open, he
encountered resistance, and the door stopped with a thudding
sound as it reached the halfway point. In a low tone, Warner
described his discovery, "They forgot something. Really ...
someone." Eddie Sorrel's body had obstructed Warner's entry.
The blood trickled down the side of Sorrel's head from what, at
first glance, seemed to be a self inflicted wound. The gun was
still clenched in the stiffened hand. Jeffry's cell phone buzzed.
"Investigator Jeffry!" he voiced into the device. Jeffry stood
there, looking at the two other fellows, nodding as he said
"yes ... OK ... yes." He pulled the phone away from his ear and
clicked the connection off.

"Amigo, my experts say your pictures are good. At least, they say, the photos came from the camera you supplied, and are valid pictures that you took of ... something." Warner frowned, "We don't really have probable cause, even with this. They might be authentic pictures, but that doesn't mean they came from ASICS." Jeffry shook his head in agreement. "We do have a way to get it."

Rat Tour Two

The guards at ASICS were not happy with the city sewer crew, who had come, unannounced, to run some "tests" on the drain. It seems that some very nasty chemical affluent had been detected coming from the area, and they had to verify or discredit the claim. Just city business. Had to be done. A disgruntled Peterson stood next to the opening as the city guys ran the probe into the hole. Up and up it went, as it uncoiled from the motorized reel. Standing on the other side of the opening, and watching over the shoulder of the operator of the probe, was Jeffry. The small video display showed the progress of the probe, and something else as well. The fresh, bright metallic glitter of the broken rod ends of the animal gates were visible. Jeffry picked up his phone, and whispered into it. "We have probable cause."

Wind Down

The orderlies had put Miguel in with the others. Miguel's fate would wait. The orderlies locked the door and left the threesome inside of the room. Had the orderlies remained, they would have been witness to a reunion of lovers. They would have observed the unleashing of a shower of breathtaking kisses, hugs, and squeezes that only those who are madly in love can give one another. Miguel and Valerie would celebrate their reunion more fully at a later time. The sound of gunfire would be cause for them to put their futures temporarily on hold. At first, the sounds seemed to be far away. There were a few shots, and then a long pause, and then a few more. It was difficult to say, for sure, which direction the gunfire was coming from, but the sounds meant only one thing to the occupant's of the room that had been Valerie's little jail. Domingo was coming! And he was bringing help - armed help. Miguel described the situation, as it had unfolded in the days and hours before. "I didn't know if he would be able to pull it off. Somebody believed him, thank God."

The feds found the door to their jail and unlocked it. Eventually, the initial investigation would disclose the location where *the drug* was stored, and the appropriate doses of the antidote would save Valerie and Jorge from the fate of all those poor people who had occupied the beds.

Only a few of the criminals had bothered to fight. In the end, Mr. B died in a hail of federal bullets, while Peterson took his own life as his complex in building B was overrun by black swathed swat units.

As news of the crime and the discovery spread, so too did the fortunes of the illegal immigrants. Domingo, Jorge, Miguel, and all the others at the farm were given indefinite stays of deportation proceedings. Peter was sent to another kind of farm, in upstate New York. Peter's new farmhouse featured the big bars of the penitentiary. In the press, the talking heads debated the ethics of using the large stockpile of *the drug*, and of the technology that produced it. Of course, new research was begun immediately to find an alternative way to produce the drug without the toll of human lives. Still, the talking heads debated the issue endlessly.

Maria had taken a job at Ed's Taco Villa. One day, not long

after the liberation, a customer walked up to her counter. He held his head down, and his hat obscured his face. "How may I help you?" she asked. The young man looked up. Smiling, Jorge said, "Well, you might let me buy your dinner."

A Few Reflections

Write what is in your heart, so long as you understand that it is good. Pray ye that it is good, and not evil, so that it brings the light and not the darkness of the draught that would extinguish it.

Alphabetical Index

Other books by this author:

Writing Internet Servers in C and C++

(ISBN 978-0-9849656-0-1)

The Drug (as separate ebook)

(ISBN 978-0-9849656-1-8)

Beelzebub's Bargain (paper digest format)

(ISBN 978-0-9849656-2-5)

Beelzebub's Bargain (ebook format)

(ISBN 978-0-9849656-3-2)

Before The Fifth Season (discontinued)

(ISBN 978-0-9849656-5-6)

www.ingramcontent.com/pod-product-compliance
Lightning Source LLC
Chambersburg PA
CBHW031505270326
41930CB00006B/255